The Poetry Of Charlotte Smith

Charlotte Turner Smith was born on May 4th 1749 in London. Her early years were dominated by her mother's early death and her father's reckless spending. Charlotte together with her younger brother and sister, Nicholas and Catherine Ann, were then raised by their maternal aunt Lucy Towers whilst their Father was away.

At age six, Charlotte went to school in Chichester and two years later moved to London with her aunt and sister where she attended a girls school in Kensington learning to dance, draw act and play music.

Upon her Father's return to England he encountered financial problems and sold off much of the family holdings before marrying the wealthy Henrietta Meriton in 1765.

At 12 Charlotte left school to be tutored at home.

On 23 February 1765, at the age of fifteen, she married Benjamin Smith, the son of Richard Smith, a wealthy West Indian merchant and a director of the East India Company. The proposal was accepted for her by her father. Charlotte was later to write that she now become a "legal prostitute". Benjamin was violent and unfaithful and had no confidence in her writings that she begun to spend more time on.

In 1766, Charlotte and Benjamin had their first child, who died the next year just days after the birth of their second. Between 1767 and 1785, the couple had ten more children.

Charlotte assisted in the family business, helping Richard Smith with his correspondence. Convincing Richard to set Benjamin up as a gentleman farmer in Hampshire she lived with him at Lys Farm from 1774 until 1783. Worried about Charlotte's future and that of his grandchildren due to his son's irresponsible ways, Richard left most of his property to Charlotte's children. However, having drawn up the will himself, it contained legal problems. The inheritance, originally worth nearly £36,000, was tied up after his death in 1776 for almost forty years.

In fact, Benjamin had already illegally spent much of it which contributed to him ending up in King's Bench Prison in December 1783. Smith moved in with him and it was here that she wrote and published her first work, Elegiac Sonnets (1784). It was an instant success, allowing Charlotte to pay for their release from prison. Smith's sonnets helped promote a revival of the form.

After their release from prison, the family moved to Dieppe, France to avoid further creditors. In 1784 she began to translate works from French into English. In 1787 she published The Romance of Real Life.

In 1785, the family returned to England locating in Sussex. Charlotte's marriage did not improve and on 15 April 1787 she left him. She wrote that she might "have been contented to reside in the same house with him", had not "his temper been so capricious and often so cruel" that her "life was not safe".

In leaving she failed to secure a legal agreement that would protect her finances. Under English primogeniture laws. Charlotte knew that her children's future rested on a successful settlement of the lawsuit over her father-in-law's will, and made every effort to earn enough to fund the suit and retain their status.

Charlotte published all her works under her own name which was considered unusual at the time. Moving to Chichester she began to write novels believing she could earn more from their sale. Her first novel, Emmeline in 1788, was a success, selling 1500 copies within months. In the next decade she wrote nine more: Ethelinde in 1789, Celestina in 1791, Desmond in 1792, The Old Manor House in 1793 – widely considered her best work, The Wanderings of Warwick in 1794, The Banished Man in 1794, Montalbert in 1795, Marchmont in 1796, and The Young Philosopher in 1798.

Charlotte's experiences caused her to promote legal reforms that would grant women more rights, making the case for these reforms through her novels. Her novel's stories showed the "legal, economic, and sexual exploitation" of women by marriage and property laws.

However her finances were a continuing concern and she moved frequently to avoid being snared. Her health was also in decline.

After her last novel and its only mild success she explored other areas include drama, children's works and a History of England. She also returned to writing poetry and Beachy Head and Other Poems was published posthumously in 1807.

Publishers did not pay as much for these works, however, and by 1803, Smith was again poverty-stricken.

Charlotte complained of gout for many years, which made it increasingly difficult and painful for her to write. By the end of her life, it had almost paralyzed her.

On 23 February 1806, her husband died in a debtors' prison and Smith finally received some of the money he owed her, but she was too ill to do anything with it.

Charlotte died on October 28th 1806, at Tilford. She is buried at Stoke Church, Stoke Park, near Guildford.

Perhaps she is best remembered by this quote from William Wordsworth who says in an essay that Smith was a poet "to whom English verse is under greater obligations than are likely to be either acknowledged or remembered"

Index Of Poems

Written Near A Port On A Dark Evening

Huge vapours brood above the clifted shore,
Night on the ocean settles dark and mute,
Save where is heard the repercussive roar
Of drowsy billows on the rugged foot
Of rocks remote; or still more distant tone
Of seamen in the anchored bark that tell
The watch relieved; or one deep voice alone
Singing the hour, and bidding "Strike the bell!"

All is black shadow but the lucid line
Marked by the light surf on the level sand,
Or where afar the ship-lights faintly shine
Like wandering fairy fires, that oft on land
Misled the pilgrim, such the dubious ray
That wavering reason lends in life's long darkling way.

A Walk In The Shrubbery
To the Cistus or Rock Rose, a beautiful plant, whose flowers
expand, and fall off twice in twenty-four hours.

The Florists, who have fondly watch'd,
Some curious bulb from hour to hour,
And, to ideal charms attach'd,
Derive their glory from a flower;
Or they, who lose in crouded rooms,
Spring's tepid suns and balmy air,
And value Flora's fairest blooms,
But in proportion as they're rare;

Feel not the pensive pleasures known
To him, who, thro' the morning mist,
Explores the bowery shrubs new blown,
A moralizing Botanist.
He marks, with colours how profuse
Some are design'd to please the eye;
While beauty some combine with use,
In admirable harmony.
The fruit buds, shadow'd red and white,
Amid young leaves of April hue;
Convey sensations of delight,
And promise fruits autumnal too:

And, while the Thrush his home and food,
Hails, as the flowering thorns unfold,
And from its trunk of ebon wood,
Rears Cytisus its floating gold;
The Lilac, whose tall head discloses
Groups of such bright empurpled shade,
And snow-globes form'd of elfin roses,
Seem for exclusive beauty made:
Such too art thou; when light anew
Above the eastern hill is seen,
Thy buds, as fearful of the dew,
Still wear their sheltering veil of green.

But in the next more genial hour
Thy tender rose-shaped cups unfold,
And soon appears the perfect flower,
With ruby spots and threads of gold.
That short and fleeting hour gone by,
And even the slightest breath of air,
Scarce heard among thy leaves to sigh,
Or little bird that flutters there;
Shakes off thy petals thin and frail,
And soon, like half-congealing snow,
The sport of every wandering gale,
They strew the humid turf below.

Yet tho' thy gauzy bells fall fast,
Long ere appears the evening crescent;
Another bloom succeeds the last,
As lovely and as evanescent.
Not so the poet's favourite Rose,
She blooms beyond a second day,
And even some later beauty shews
Some charm still lingering in decay.
Thus those, who thro' life's path have pass'd,
A path how seldom strewn with flowers !
May have met Friendships formed to last
Beyond the noonday's golden hours.

While quickly formed, dissolv'd as soon,
Some warm attachments I have known
Just flourish for an hour at noon,
But leave no trace when overblown.
Minds that form these, with ardent zeal
Their new connexions fondly cherish,
And for a moment keenly feel
Affection, doomed as soon to perish;
Incapable of Friendship long,
Awake to every new impression,
Old friends, becoming ci-devant !
Are still replaced by a Succession.

Apostrophe
To An Old Tree.

Where thy broad branches brave the bitter North,
Like rugged, indigent, unheeded, worth,
Lo! Vegetation's guardian hands emboss
Each giant limb with fronds of studded moss,
That clothes the bark in many a fringed fold
Begemm'd with scarlet shields, and cups of gold,
Which, to the wildest winds their webs oppose,
And mock the arrowy sleet, or weltering snows.
But to the warmer West the woodbine fair
With tassels that perfumed the summer air,
The mantling clematis, whose feathery bowers
Waved in festoons with nightshade's purple flowers,
The silver weed, whose corded fillets wove
Round thy pale rind, even as deceitful love
Of mercenary beauty would engage
The dotard fondness of decrepit age;
All these, that during summer's halcyon days
With their green canopies conceal'd thy sprays,
Are gone for ever; or disfigured, trail
Their sallow relicts in the autumnal gale;
Or o'er thy roots, in faded fragments toss'd,
But tell of happier hours, and sweetness lost!

Thus in Fate's trying hour, when furious storms
Strip social life of Pleasure's fragile forms,
And awful Justice , as his rightful prey
Tears Luxury's silk, and jewel'd robe, away,
While reads Adversity her lesson stern,
And Fortune's minions tremble as they learn;
The crowds around her gilded car that hung,
Bent the lithe knee, and troul'd the honey'd tongue,
Desponding fall, or fly in pale despair;
And Scorn alone remembers that they were.
Not so Integrity ; unchanged he lives
In the rude armour conscious Honour gives,
And dares with hardy front the troubled sky,
In Honesty's uninjured panoply.
Ne'er on Prosperity's enfeebling bed
Or rosy pillows, he reposed his head,

But given to useful arts, his ardent mind
Has sought the general welfare of mankind;
To mitigate their ills his greatest bliss,
While studying them , has taught him what he is ;
He , when the human tempest rages worst,
And the earth shudders as the thunders burst,
Firm, as thy northern branch, is rooted fast,
And if he can't avert , endures the blast.

April
Green o'er the copses spring's soft hues are spreading,
High wave the reeds in the transparent floods,
The oak its sear and sallow foliage shedding,
From their moss'd cradles start its infant buds.
Pale as the tranquil tide of summer's ocean,
The willow now its slender leaf unveils;
And through the sky with swiftly fleeting motion,
Driv'n by the wind, the rack of April sails.
Then, as the gust declines, the stealing showers
Fall fresh and noiseless; while at closing day
The low sun gleams on moist and half-blown flowers,
That promise garlands for approaching May.
Bless'd are yon peasant children, simply singing,
Who through the new-sprung grass rejoicing rove;
More bless'd! to whom the time , fond thought is bringing,
Of friends expected, or returning love.
The pensive wanderer bless'd, to whom reflection
Points out some future views that soothe his mind;
Me how unlike! whom cruel recollection
But tells of comfort I shall never find!

Hope, that on Nature's youth is still attending,
No more to me her syren song shall sing;
Never to me her influence extending,

Shall I again enjoy the days of Spring!
Yet, how I loved them once these scenes remind me,
When light of heart, in childhood's thoughtless mirth,
I reck'd not that the cruel lot assign'd me
Should make me curse the hour that gave me birth!
Then, from thy wild-wood banks, Aruna! roving,
Thy thymy downs with sportive steps I sought,
And Nature's charms, with artless transport loving,
Sung, like the birds, unheeded and untaught.
But now the springtide's pleasant hours returning,
Serve to awaken me to sharper pain;
Recalling scenes of agony and mourning,
Of baffled hope and prayers preferr'd in vain.
Thus shone the sun, his vernal rays displaying,
Thus did the woods in early verdure wave,
While dire disease on all I loved was preying,
And flowers seem'd rising but to strew her grave.
Now, 'mid reviving blooms, I coldly languish,
Spring seems devoid of joy to me alone;
Each sound of pleasure aggravates my anguish,
And speaks of beauty, youth, and sweetness gone.
Yet, as stern duty bids, with faint endeavour
I drag on life, contending with my woe,
Though conscious misery still repeats, that never
My soul one pleasurable hour shall know.
Lost in the tomb, when Hope no more appeases
The fester'd wounds that prompt the eternal sigh,
Grief, the most fatal of the heart's diseases,
Soon teaches, whom it fastens on, to die.

The wretch undone, for pain alone existing,
The abject dread of death shall sure subdue,
And far from his decisive hand resisting,
Rejoice to bid a world like this, adieu.

Beachy Head
On thy stupendous summit, rock sublime !
That o'er the channel rear'd, half way at sea
The mariner at early morning hails,
I would recline; while Fancy should go forth,
And represent the strange and awful hour
Of vast concussion; when the Omnipotent
Stretch'd forth his arm, and rent the solid hills,
Bidding the impetuous main flood rush between

The rifted shores, and from the continent
Eternally divided this green isle.
Imperial lord of the high southern coast !
From thy projecting head-land I would mark
Far in the east the shades of night disperse,
Melting and thinned, as from the dark blue wave

Emerging, brilliant rays of arrowy light
Dart from the horizon; when the glorious sun
Just lifts above it his resplendent orb.
Advances now, with feathery silver touched,
The rippling tide of flood; glisten the sands,
While, inmates of the chalky clefts that scar
Thy sides precipitous, with shrill harsh cry,
Their white wings glancing in the level beam,
The terns, and gulls, and tarrocks, seek their food,
And thy rough hollows echo to the voice

Of the gray choughs, and ever restless daws,
With clamour, not unlike the chiding hounds,
While the lone shepherd, and his baying dog,
Drive to thy turfy crest his bleating flock.
The high meridian of the day is past,
And Ocean now, reflecting the calm Heaven,
Is of cerulean hue; and murmurs low
The tide of ebb, upon the level sands.
The sloop, her angular canvas shifting still,
Catches the light and variable airs
That but a little crisp the summer sea.
Dimpling its tranquil surface.
Afar off,
And just emerging from the arch immense

Where seem to part the elements, a fleet
Of fishing vessels stretch their lesser sails;
While more remote, and like a dubious spot
Just hanging in the horizon, laden deep,
The ship of commerce richly freighted, makes
Her slower progress, on her distant voyage,
Bound to the orient climates, where the sun
Matures the spice within its odorous shell,
And, rivalling the gray worm's filmy toil,
Bursts from its pod the vegetable down;
Which in long turban'd wreaths, from torrid heat
Defends the brows of Asia's countless casts.
There the Earth hides within her glowing breast
The beamy adamant, and the round pearl
Enchased in rugged covering; which the slave,
With perilous and breathless toil, tears off

From the rough sea-rock, deep beneath the waves.
These are the toys of Nature; and her sport
Of little estimate in Reason's eye:
And they who reason, with abhorrence see
Man, for such gaudes and baubles, violate
The sacred freedom of his fellow man
Erroneous estimate ! As Heaven's pure air,
Fresh as it blows on this aërial height,
Or sound of seas upon the stony strand,

Or inland, the gay harmony of birds,
And winds that wander in the leafy woods;
Are to the unadulterate taste more worth
Than the elaborate harmony, brought out
From fretted stop, or modulated airs
Of vocal science.So the brightest gems,
Glancing resplendent on the regal crown,

Or trembling in the high born beauty's ear,
Are poor and paltry, to the lovely light
Of the fair star, that as the day declines,
Attendant on her queen, the crescent moon,
Bathes her bright tresses in the eastern wave.
For now the sun is verging to the sea,
And as he westward sinks, the floating clouds
Suspended, move upon the evening gale,
And gathering round his orb, as if to shade
The insufferable brightness, they resign
Their gauzy whiteness; and more warm'd, assume
All hues of purple. There, transparent gold
Mingles with ruby tints, and sapphire gleams,
And colours, such as Nature through her works
Shews only in the ethereal canopy.
Thither aspiring Fancy fondly soars,

Wandering sublime thro' visionary vales,
Where bright pavilions rise, and trophies, fann'd
By airs celestial; and adorn'd with wreaths
Of flowers that bloom amid elysian bowers.
Now bright, and brighter still the colours glow,
Till half the lustrous orb within the flood
Seems to retire: the flood reflecting still
Its splendor, and in mimic glory drest;
Till the last ray shot upward, fires the clouds
With blazing crimson; then in paler light,
Long lines of tenderer radiance, lingering yield
To partial darkness; and on the opposing side
The early moon distinctly rising, throws
Her pearly brilliance on the trembling tide.

The fishermen, who at set seasons pass
Many a league off at sea their toiling night,
Now hail their comrades, from their daily task
Returning; and make ready for their own,
With the night tide commencing:The night tide
Bears a dark vessel on, whose hull and sails
Mark her a coaster from the north. Her keel
Now ploughs the sand; and sidelong now she leans,
While with loud clamours her athletic crew
Unload her; and resounds the busy hum
Along the wave-worn rocks. Yet more remote,
Where the rough cliff hangs beetling o'er its base,

All breathes repose; the water's rippling sound
Scarce heard; but now and then the sea-snipe's cry
Just tells that something living is abroad;
And sometimes crossing on the moonbright line,

Glimmers the skiff, faintly discern'd awhile,
Then lost in shadow.
Contemplation here,
High on her throne of rock, aloof may sit,
And bid recording Memory unfold
Her scroll voluminousbid her retrace
The period, when from Neustria's hostile shore
The Norman launch'd his galleys, and the bay
O'er which that mass of ruin frowns even now
In vain and sullen menace, then received
The new invaders; a proud martial race,
Of Scandinavia the undaunted sons,
Whom Dogon, Fier-a-bras, and Humfroi led
To conquest: while Trinacria to their power
Yielded her wheaten garland; and when thou,

Parthenope ! within thy fertile bay
Receiv'd the victors
In the mailed ranks
Of Normans landing on the British coast
Rode Taillefer; and with astounding voice
Thunder'd the war song daring Roland sang
First in the fierce contention: vainly brave,
One not inglorious struggle England made
But failing, saw the Saxon heptarchy
Finish for ever.Then the holy pile,
Yet seen upon the field of conquest, rose,
Where to appease heaven's wrath for so much blood,
The conqueror bade unceasing prayers ascend,
And requiems for the slayers and the slain.
But let not modern Gallia form from hence

Presumptuous hopes, that ever thou again,
Queen of the isles ! shalt crouch to foreign arms.
The enervate sons of Italy may yield;
And the Iberian, all his trophies torn
And wrapp'd in Superstition's monkish weed,
May shelter his abasement, and put on
Degrading fetters. Never, never thou !
Imperial mistress of the obedient sea;
But thou, in thy integrity secure,
Shalt now undaunted meet a world in arms.
England ! 'twas where this promontory rears
Its rugged brow above the channel wave,
Parting the hostile nations, that thy fame,
Thy naval fame was tarnish'd, at what time
Thou, leagued with the Batavian, gavest to France

One day of triumphtriumph the more loud,
Because even then so rare. Oh ! well redeem'd,
Since, by a series of illustrious men,
Such as no other country ever rear'd,
To vindicate her cause. It is a list
Which, as Fame echoes it, blanches the cheek
Of bold Ambition; while the despot feels
The extorted sceptre tremble in his grasp.
From even the proudest roll by glory fill'd,
How gladly the reflecting mind returns
To simple scenes of peace and industry,
Where, bosom'd in some valley of the hills
Stands the lone farm; its gate with tawny ricks
Surrounded, and with granaries and sheds,
Roof'd with green mosses, and by elms and ash

Partially shaded; and not far remov'd
The hut of sea-flints built; the humble home
Of one, who sometimes watches on the heights,
When hid in the cold mist of passing clouds,
The flock, with dripping fleeces, are dispers'd
O'er the wide down; then from some ridged point
That overlooks the sea, his eager eye
Watches the bark that for his signal waits
To land its merchandize:Quitting for this
Clandestine traffic his more honest toil,
The crook abandoning, he braves himself
The heaviest snow-storm of December's night,
When with conflicting winds the ocean raves,
And on the tossing boat, unfearing mounts
To meet the partners of the perilous trade,
And share their hazard. Well it were for him,

If no such commerce of destruction known,
He were content with what the earth affords
To human labour; even where she seems
Reluctant most. More happy is the hind,
Who, with his own hands rears on some black moor,
Or turbary, his independent hut
Cover'd with heather, whence the slow white smoke
Of smouldering peat arisesA few sheep,
His best possession, with his children share
The rugged shed when wintry tempests blow;
But, when with Spring's return the green blades rise
Amid the russet heath, the household live
Joint tenants of the waste throughout the day,
And often, from her nest, among the swamps,
Where the gemm'd sun-dew grows, or fring'd buck-bean,
They scare the plover, that with plaintive cries

Flutters, as sorely wounded, down the wind.

Rude, and but just remov'd from savage life
Is the rough dweller among scenes like these,
(Scenes all unlike the poet's fabling dreams
Describing Arcady)But he is free;
The dread that follows on illegal acts
He never feels; and his industrious mate
Shares in his labour. Where the brook is traced
By crouding osiers, and the black coot hides
Among the plashy reeds, her diving brood,
The matron wades; gathering the long green rush
That well prepar'd hereafter lends its light
To her poor cottage, dark and cheerless else
Thro' the drear hours of Winter. Otherwhile
She leads her infant group where charlock grows
'Unprofitably gay,' or to the fields,

Where congregate the linnet and the finch,
That on the thistles, so profusely spread,
Feast in the desert; the poor family
Early resort, extirpating with care
These, and the gaudier mischief of the ground;
Then flames the high rais'd heap; seen afar off
Like hostile war-fires flashing to the sky.
Another task is theirs: On fields that shew
As angry Heaven had rain'd sterility,
Stony and cold, and hostile to the plough,
Where clamouring loud, the evening curlew runs
And drops her spotted eggs among the flints;
The mother and the children pile the stones
In rugged pyramids;and all this toil
They patiently encounter; well content
On their flock bed to slumber undisturb'd

Beneath the smoky roof they call their own.
Oh ! little knows the sturdy hind, who stands
Gazing, with looks where envy and contempt
Are often strangely mingled, on the car
Where prosperous Fortune sits; what secret care
Or sick satiety is often hid,
Beneath the splendid outside: He knows not
How frequently the child of Luxury
Enjoying nothing, flies from place to place
In chase of pleasure that eludes his grasp;
And that content is e'en less found by him,
Than by the labourer, whose pick-axe smooths
The road before his chariot; and who doffs
What was an hat; and as the train pass on,
Thinks how one day's expenditure, like this,

Would cheer him for long months, when to his toil
The frozen earth closes her marble breast.
Ah ! who is happy? Happiness! a word

That like false fire, from marsh effluvia born,
Misleads the wanderer, destin'd to contend
In the world's wilderness, with want or woe
Yet they are happy, who have never ask'd
What good or evil means. The boy
That on the river's margin gaily plays,
Has heard that Death is there. He knows not Death,
And therefore fears it not; and venturing in
He gains a bullrush, or a minnowthen,
At certain peril, for a worthless prize,
A crow's, or raven's nest, he climbs the boll,

Of some tall pine; and of his prowess proud,
Is for a moment happy. Are your cares,
Ye who despise him, never worse applied?
The village girl is happy, who sets forth
To distant fair, gay in her Sunday suit,
With cherry colour'd knots, and flourish'd shawl,
And bonnet newly purchas'd. So is he
Her little brother, who his mimic drum
Beats, till he drowns her rural lovers' oaths
Of constant faith, and still increasing love;
Ah ! yet a while, and half those oaths believ'd,
Her happiness is vanish'd; and the boy
While yet a stripling, finds the sound he lov'd
Has led him on, till he has given up
His freedom, and his happiness together.

I once was happy, when while yet a child,
I learn'd to love these upland solitudes,
And, when elastic as the mountain air,
To my light spirit, care was yet unknown
And evil unforeseen:Early it came,
And childhood scarcely passed, I was condemned,
A guiltless exile, silently to sigh,
While Memory, with faithful pencil, drew
The contrast; and regretting, I compar'd
With the polluted smoky atmosphere
And dark and stifling streets, the southern hills
That to the setting Sun, their graceful heads
Rearing, o'erlook the frith, where Vecta breaks
With her white rocks, the strong impetuous tide,
When western winds the vast Atlantic urge
To thunder on the coastHaunts of my youth!

Scenes of fond day dreams, I behold ye yet!
Where 'twas so pleasant by thy northern slopes
To climb the winding sheep-path, aided oft
By scatter'd thorns: whose spiny branches bore
Small woolly tufts, spoils of the vagrant lamb
There seeking shelter from the noon-day sun;
And pleasant, seated on the short soft turf,

To look beneath upon the hollow way
While heavily upward mov'd the labouring wain,
And stalking slowly by, the sturdy hind
To ease his panting team, stopp'd with a stone
The grating wheel.
Advancing higher still
The prospect widens, and the village church
But little, o'er the lowly roofs around

Rears its gray belfry, and its simple vane;
Those lowly roofs of thatch are half conceal'd
By the rude arms of trees, lovely in spring,
When on each bough, the rosy-tinctur'd bloom
Sits thick, and promises autumnal plenty.
For even those orchards round the Norman farms,
Which, as their owners mark the promis'd fruit,
Console them for the vineyards of the south,
Surpass not these.
Where woods of ash, and beech,
And partial copses, fringe the green hill foot,
The upland shepherd rears his modest home,
There wanders by, a little nameless stream
That from the hill wells forth, bright now and clear,
Or after rain with chalky mixture gray,

But still refreshing in its shallow course,
The cottage garden; most for use design'd,
Yet not of beauty destitute. The vine
Mantles the little casement; yet the briar
Drops fragrant dew among the July flowers;
And pansies rayed, and freak'd and mottled pinks
Grow among balm, and rosemary and rue:
There honeysuckles flaunt, and roses blow
Almost uncultured: Some with dark green leaves
Contrast their flowers of pure unsullied white;
Others, like velvet robes of regal state
Of richest crimson, while in thorny moss
Enshrined and cradled, the most lovely, wear
The hues of youthful beauty's glowing cheek.
With fond regret I recollect e'en now
In Spring and Summer, what delight I felt

Among these cottage gardens, and how much
Such artless nosegays, knotted with a rush
By village housewife or her ruddy maid,
Were welcome to me; soon and simply pleas'd.
An early worshipper at Nature's shrine;
I loved her rudest scenes—warrens, and heaths,
And yellow commons, and birch-shaded hollows,
And hedge rows, bordering unfrequented lanes
Bowered with wild roses, and the clasping woodbine
Where purple tassels of the tangling vetch

With bittersweet, and bryony inweave,
And the dew fills the silver bindweed's cups
I loved to trace the brooks whose humid banks
Nourish the harebell, and the freckled pagil;
And stroll among o'ershadowing woods of beech,

Lending in Summer, from the heats of noon
A whispering shade; while haply there reclines
Some pensive lover of uncultur'd flowers,
Who, from the tumps with bright green mosses clad,
Plucks the wood sorrel, with its light thin leaves,
Heart-shaped, and triply folded; and its root
Creeping like beaded coral; or who there
Gathers, the copse's pride, anémones,
With rays like golden studs on ivory laid
Most delicate: but touch'd with purple clouds,
Fit crown for April's fair but changeful brow.
Ah ! hills so early loved ! in fancy still
I breathe your pure keen air; and still behold
Those widely spreading views, mocking alike
The Poet and the Painter's utmost art.

And still, observing objects more minute,
Wondering remark the strange and foreign forms
Of sea-shells; with the pale calcareous soil
Mingled, and seeming of resembling substance.
Tho' surely the blue Ocean (from the heights
Where the downs westward trend, but dimly seen)
Here never roll'd its surge. Does Nature then
Mimic, in wanton mood, fantastic shapes
Of bivalves, and inwreathed volutes, that cling
To the dark sea-rock of the wat'ry world ?
Or did this range of chalky mountains, once
Form a vast bason, where the Ocean waves
Swell'd fathomless ? What time these fossil shells,
Buoy'd on their native element, were thrown
Among the imbedding calx: when the huge hill
Its giant bulk heaved, and in strange ferment

Grew up a guardian barrier, 'twixt the sea
And the green level of the sylvan weald.
Ah ! very vain is Science' proudest boast,
And but a little light its flame yet lends
To its most ardent votaries; since from whence
These fossil forms are seen, is but conjecture,
Food for vague theories, or vain dispute,
While to his daily task the peasant goes,
Unheeding such inquiry; with no care
But that the kindly change of sun and shower,
Fit for his toil the earth he cultivates.
As little recks the herdsman of the hill,
Who on some turfy knoll, idly reclined,

Watches his wether flock; that deep beneath
Rest the remains of men, of whom is left

No traces in the records of mankind,
Save what these half obliterated mounds
And half fill'd trenches doubtfully impart
To some lone antiquary; who on times remote,
Since which two thousand years have roll'd away,
Loves to contemplate. He perhaps may trace,
Or fancy he can trace, the oblong square
Where the mail'd legions, under Claudius, rear'd,
The rampire, or excavated fossé delved;
What time the huge unwieldy Elephant
Auxiliary reluctant, hither led,
From Afric's forest glooms and tawny sands,
First felt the Northern blast, and his vast frame
Sunk useless; whence in after ages found,
The wondering hinds, on those enormous bones
Gaz'd; and in giants dwelling on the hills
Believed and marvell'd

Hither, Ambition, come!
Come and behold the nothingness of all
For which you carry thro' the oppressed Earth,
War, and its train of horrorssee where tread
The innumerous hoofs of flocks above the works
By which the warrior sought to register
His glory, and immortalize his name
The pirate Dane, who from his circular camp
Bore in destructive robbery, fire and sword
Down thro' the vale, sleeps unremember'd here;
And here, beneath the green sward, rests alike
The savage native, who his acorn meal
Shar'd with the herds, that ranged the pathless woods;
And the centurion, who on these wide hills
Encamping, planted the Imperial Eagle.
All, with the lapse of Time, have passed away,

Even as the clouds, with dark and dragon shapes,
Or like vast promontories crown'd with towers,
Cast their broad shadows on the downs: then sail
Far to the northward, and their transient gloom
Is soon forgotten.
But from thoughts like these,
By human crimes suggested, let us turn
To where a more attractive study courts
The wanderer of the hills; while shepherd girls
Will from among the fescue bring him flowers,
Of wonderous mockery; some resembling bees
In velvet vest, intent on their sweet toil,
While others mimic flies, that lightly sport
In the green shade, or float along the pool,

But here seem perch'd upon the slender stalk,

And gathering honey dew. While in the breeze
That wafts the thistle's plumed seed along,
Blue bells wave tremulous. The mountain thyme
Purples the hassock of the heaving mole,
And the short turf is gay with tormentil,
And bird's foot trefoil, and the lesser tribes
Of hawkweed; spangling it with fringed stars.
Near where a richer tract of cultur'd land
Slopes to the south; and burnished by the sun,
Bend in the gale of August, floods of corn;
The guardian of the flock, with watchful care,
Repels by voice and dog the encroaching sheep
While his boy visits every wired trap
That scars the turf; and from the pit-falls takes
The timid migrants, who from distant wilds,
Warrens, and stone quarries, are destined thus

To lose their short existence. But unsought
By Luxury yet, the Shepherd still protects
The social bird, who from his native haunts
Of willowy current, or the rushy pool,
Follows the fleecy croud, and flirts and skims,
In fellowship among them.
Where the knoll
More elevated takes the changeful winds,
The windmill rears its vanes; and thitherward
With his white load, the master travelling,
Scares the rooks rising slow on whispering wings,
While o'er his head, before the summer sun
Lights up the blue expanse, heard more than seen,
The lark sings matins; and above the clouds
Floating, embathes his spotted breast in dew.

Beneath the shadow of a gnarled thorn,
Bent by the sea blast, from a seat of turf
With fairy nosegays strewn, how wide the view !
Till in the distant north it melts away,
And mingles indiscriminate with clouds:
But if the eye could reach so far, the mart
Of England's capital, its domes and spires
Might be perceivedYet hence the distant range
Of Kentish hills, appear in purple haze;
And nearer, undulate the wooded heights,
And airy summits, that above the mole
Rise in green beauty; and the beacon'd ridge
Of Black-down shagg'd with heath, and swelling rude
Like a dark island from the vale; its brow
Catching the last rays of the evening sun
That gleam between the nearer park's old oaks,

Then lighten up the river, and make prominent
The portal, and the ruin'd battlements
Of that dismantled fortress; rais'd what time
The Conqueror's successors fiercely fought,
Tearing with civil feuds the desolate land.
But now a tiller of the soil dwells there,
And of the turret's loop'd and rafter'd halls
Has made an humbler homesteadWhere he sees,
Instead of armed foemen, herds that graze
Along his yellow meadows; or his flocks
At evening from the upland driv'n to fold
In such a castellated mansion once
A stranger chose his home; and where hard by
In rude disorder fallen, and hid with brushwood
Lay fragments gray of towers and buttresses,

Among the ruins, often he would muse
His rustic meal soon ended, he was wont
To wander forth, listening the evening sounds
Of rushing milldam, or the distant team,
Or night-jar, chasing fern-flies: the tir'd hind
Pass'd him at nightfall, wondering he should sit
On the hill top so late: they from the coast
Who sought bye paths with their clandestine load,
Saw with suspicious doubt, the lonely man
Cross on their way: but village maidens thought
His senses injur'd; and with pity say
That he, poor youth ! must have been cross'd in love
For often, stretch'd upon the mountain turf
With folded arms, and eyes intently fix'd
Where ancient elms and firs obscured a grange,
Some little space within the vale below,

They heard him, as complaining of his fate,
And to the murmuring wind, of cold neglect
And baffled hope he told.The peasant girls
These plaintive sounds remember, and even now
Among them may be heard the stranger's songs.
Were I a Shepherd on the hill
And ever as the mists withdrew
Could see the willows of the rill
Shading the footway to the mill
Where once I walk'd with you

And as away Night's shadows sail,
And sounds of birds and brooks arise,
Believe, that from the woody vale
I hear your voice upon the gale
In soothing melodies;
And viewing from the Alpine height,
The prospect dress'd in hues of air,
Could say, while transient colours bright

Touch'd the fair scene with dewy light,
'Tis, that her eyes are there !
I think, I could endure my lot
And linger on a few short years,
And then, by all but you forgot,
Sleep, where the turf that clothes the spot
May claim some pitying tears.

For 'tis not easy to forget
One, who thro' life has lov'd you still,
And you, however late, might yet
With sighs to Memory giv'n, regret
The Shepherd of the Hill.
Yet otherwhile it seem'd as if young Hope
Her flattering pencil gave to Fancy's hand,
And in his wanderings, rear'd to sooth his soul
Ideal bowers of pleasureThen, of Solitude
And of his hermit life, still more enamour'd,
His home was in the forest; and wild fruits

And bread sustain'd him. There in early spring
The Barkmen found him, e'er the sun arose;
There at their daily toil, the Wedgecutters
Beheld him thro' the distant thicket move.
The shaggy dog following the truffle hunter,
Bark'd at the loiterer; and perchance at night
Belated villagers from fair or wake,
While the fresh night-wind let the moonbeams in
Between the swaying boughs, just saw him pass,
And then in silence, gliding like a ghost
He vanish'd ! Lost among the deepening gloom.
But near one ancient tree, whose wreathed roots
Form'd a rude couch, love-songs and scatter'd rhymes,
Unfinish'd sentences, or half erased,
And rhapsodies like this, were sometimes found

Let us to woodland wilds repair
While yet the glittering night-dews seem
To wait the freshly-breathing air,
Precursive of the morning beam,
That rising with advancing day,
Scatters the silver drops away.
An elm, uprooted by the storm,
The trunk with mosses gray and green,
Shall make for us a rustic form,
Where lighter grows the forest scene;
And far among the bowery shades,
Are ferny lawns and grassy glades.

Retiring May to lovely June
Her latest garland now resigns;
The banks with cuckoo-flowers are strewn,

The woodwalks blue with columbines,
And with its reeds, the wandering stream
Reflects the flag-flower's golden gleam.
There, feathering down the turf to meet,
Their shadowy arms the beeches spread,
While high above our sylvan seat,
Lifts the light ash its airy head;
And later leaved, the oaks between
Extend their bows of vernal green.

The slender birch its paper rind
Seems offering to divided love,
And shuddering even without a wind
Aspins, their paler foliage move,
As if some spirit of the air
Breath'd a low sigh in passing there.
The Squirrel in his frolic mood,
Will fearless bound among the boughs;
Yaffils laugh loudly thro' the wood,
And murmuring ring-doves tell their vows;
While we, as sweetest woodscents rise,
Listen to woodland melodies.

And I'll contrive a sylvan room
Against the time of summer heat,
Where leaves, inwoven in Nature's loom,
Shall canopy our green retreat;
And gales that 'close the eye of day'
Shall linger, e'er they die away.
And when a sear and sallow hue
From early frost the bower receives,
I'll dress the sand rock cave for you,
And strew the floor with heath and leaves,
That you, against the autumnal air
May find securer shelter there.

The Nightingale will then have ceas'd
To sing her moonlight serenade;
But the gay bird with blushing breast,
And Woodlarks still will haunt the shade,
And by the borders of the spring
Reed-wrens will yet be carolling.
The forest hermit's lonely cave
None but such soothing sounds shall reach,
Or hardly heard, the distant wave
Slow breaking on the stony beach;
Or winds, that now sigh soft and low,
Now make wild music as they blow.

And then, before the chilling North
The tawny foliage falling light,
Seems, as it flits along the earth,

The footfall of the busy Sprite,
Who wrapt in pale autumnal gloom,
Calls up the mist-born Mushroom.
Oh ! could I hear your soft voice there,
And see you in the forest green
All beauteous as you are, more fair
You'd look, amid the sylvan scene,
And in a wood-girl's simple guise,
Be still more lovely in mine eyes.

Ye phantoms of unreal delight,
Visions of fond delirium born !
Rise not on my deluded sight,
Then leave me drooping and forlorn
To know, such bliss can never be,
Unless loved like me.
The visionary, nursing dreams like these,
Is not indeed unhappy. Summer woods
Wave over him, and whisper as they wave,
Some future blessings he may yet enjoy.
And as above him sail the silver clouds,
He follows them in thought to distant climes,
Where, far from the cold policy of this,

Dividing him from her he fondly loves,
He, in some island of the southern sea,
May haply build his cane-constructed bower
Beneath the bread-fruit, or aspiring palm,
With long green foliage rippling in the gale.
Oh ! let him cherish his ideal bliss
For what is life, when Hope has ceas'd to strew
Her fragile flowers along its thorny way ?
And sad and gloomy are his days, who lives
Of Hope abandon'd !
Just beneath the rock
Where Beachy overpeers the channel wave,
Within a cavern mined by wintry tides
Dwelt one, who long disgusted with the world
And all its ways, appear'd to suffer life

Rather than live; the soul-reviving gale,
Fanning the bean-field, or the thymy heath,
Had not for many summers breathed on him;
And nothing mark'd to him the season's change,
Save that more gently rose the placid sea,
And that the birds which winter on the coast
Gave place to other migrants; save that the fog,
Hovering no more above the beetling cliffs
Betray'd not then the little careless sheep
On the brink grazing, while their headlong fall
Near the lone Hermit's flint-surrounded home,
Claim'd unavailing pity; for his heart

Was feelingly alive to all that breath'd;
And outraged as he was, in sanguine youth,
By human crimes, he still acutely felt
For human misery.

Wandering on the beach,
He learn'd to augur from the clouds of heaven,
And from the changing colours of the sea,
And sullen murmurs of the hollow cliffs,
Or the dark porpoises, that near the shore
Gambol'd and sported on the level brine
When tempests were approaching: then at night
He listen'd to the wind; and as it drove
The billows with o'erwhelming vehemence
He, starting from his rugged couch, went forth
And hazarding a life, too valueless,
He waded thro' the waves, with plank or pole
Towards where the mariner in conflict dread
Was buffeting for life the roaring surge;
And now just seen, now lost in foaming gulphs,
The dismal gleaming of the clouded moon

Shew'd the dire peril. Often he had snatch'd
From the wild billows, some unhappy man
Who liv'd to bless the hermit of the rocks.
But if his generous cares were all in vain,
And with slow swell the tide of morning bore
Some blue swol'n cor'se to land; the pale recluse
Dug in the chalk a sepulchreabove
Where the dank sea-wrack mark'd the utmost tide,
And with his prayers perform'd the obsequies
For the poor helpless stranger.
One dark night
The equinoctial wind blew south by west,
Fierce on the shore; the bellowing cliffs were shook
Even to their stony base, and fragments fell
Flashing and thundering on the angry flood.

At day-break, anxious for the lonely man,
His cave the mountain shepherds visited,
Tho' sand and banks of weeds had choak'd their way
He was not in it; but his drowned cor'se
By the waves wafted, near his former home
Receiv'd the rites of burial. Those who read
Chisel'd within the rock, these mournful lines,
Memorials of his sufferings, did not grieve,
That dying in the cause of charity
His spirit, from its earthly bondage freed,
Had to some better region fled for ever.

Elegy

'Dark gathering clouds involve the threatening skies,
The sea heaves conscious of the impending gloom,
Deep, hollow murmurs from the cliffs arise;
They come, the Spirits of the Tempest come!

'Oh! may such terrors mark the approaching night
As reign'd on that these streaming eyes deplore!
Flash, ye red fires of heaven, with fatal light,
And with conflicting winds ye waters roar!
'Loud and more loud, ye foaming billows, burst!
Ye warring elements, more fiercely rave!
Till the wide waves o'erwhelm the spot accurst
'Where ruthless Avarice finds a quiet grave!' '
Thus with clasp'd hands, wild looks, and streaming hair,
While shrieks of horror broke her trembling speech,
A wretched maid, the victim of despair,
Survey'd the threatening storm and desert beech.
Then to the tomb where now the father slept
Whose rugged nature bade her sorrows flow,
Frantic she turn'd and beat her breast and wept,
Invoking vengeance on the dust below.
'Lo! rising there above each humbler heap,
Yon cypher'd stones his name and wealth relate,
Who gave his son, remorseless, to the deep,
While I, his living victim, curse my fate.
'Oh, my lost love! no tomb is placed for thee,
That may to strangers' eyes thy worth impart;
Thou hast no grave but in the stormy sea,
And no memorial but this breaking heart.
'Forth to the world, a widow'd wanderer driven,
I pour to winds and waves the unheeded tear,
Try with vain effort to submit to Heaven,
And fruitless call on him 'who cannot hear.'
'Oh! might I fondly clasp him once again,
While o'er my head the infuriate billows pour,
Forget in death this agonizing pain,
And feel his father's cruelty no more!
'Part, raging waters! part, and show beneath,
In your dread caves, his pale and mangled form;
Now, while the demons of despair and death
Ride on the blast, and urge the howling storm:

'Lo! by the lightning's momentary blaze,
I see him rise the whitening waves above,
No longer such as when in happier days
He gave the enchanted hours to me and love.
'Such, as when daring the enchafed sea,
And courting dangerous toil, he often said
That every peril, one soft smile from me,
One sigh of speechless tenderness o'erpaid.
'But dead, disfigured, while between the roar
Of the loud waves his accents pierce mine ear,

And seem to say Ah, wretch! delay no more,
But come, unhappy mourner, meet me here.
'Yet, powerful Fancy, bid the phantom stay,
Still let me hear him! 'Tis already past;
Along the waves his shadow glides away,
I lose his voice amid the deafening blast.
'Ah, wild delusion, born of frantic pain!
He hears not, comes not from his watery bed;
My tears, my anguish, my despair are vain,
The insatiate ocean gives not up its dead.
' 'Tis not his voice! Hark! the deep thunders roll;
Upheaves the ground; the rocky barriers fail;
Approach, ye horrors that delight my soul,
Despair, and Death, and Desolation, hail!'
The Ocean hears. The embodied waters come
Rise o'er the land, and with resistless sweep
Tear from its base the proud aggressor's tomb,
And bear the injured to eternal sleep.

Evening

Oh! soothing hour, when glowing day,
Low in the western wave declines,
And village murmurs die away,
And bright the vesper planet shines;
I love to hear the gale of Even
Breathing along the new-leaf'd copse,
And feel the freshening dew of Heaven,
Fall silently in limpid drops.

For, like a friend's consoling sighs,
That breeze of night to me appears;
And, as soft dew from Pity's eyes,
Descend those pure celestial tears.
Alas ! for those who long have borne,
Like me, a heart by sorrow riven,
Who, but the plaintive winds, will mourn,
What tears will fall, but those of Heaven ?

Flora

Remote from scenes, where the o'erwearied mind
Shrinks from the crimes and follies of mankind,
From hostile menace, and offensive boast,
Peace, and her train of home-born pleasures lost;
To fancy's reign, who would not gladly turn,
And lose awhile, the miseries they mourn
In sweet oblivion ? Come then, Fancy ! deign,
Queen of ideal pleasure, once again,
To lend thy magic pencil, and to bring
Such lovely forms, as in life's happier spring,

On the green margin of my native Wey,
Before mine infant eyes were wont to play,
And with that pencil, teach me to describe
The enchanting goddess of the flowery tribe,
Whose first prerogative it is to chase
The clouds that hang on languid beauty's face;
And, while advancing suns and tepid showers,
Lead on the laughing Spring's delicious hours,
Bid the wan maid the hues of health assume,
Charm with new grace, and blush with fresher bloom.
The vision comes !While slowly melt away,
Night's hovering shades before the eastern ray,
Ere yet declines the morning's humid star,
Fair Fancy brings her; in her leafy car

Flora descends, to dress the expecting earth,
Awake the germs, and call the buds to birth;
Bid each hybernacle its cell unfold,
And open silken leaves, and eyes of gold !
Of forest foliage of the firmest shade
Enwove by magic hands, the car was made;
Oak, and the ample Plane, without entwined,
And Beech and Ash the verdant concave lin'd;
The Saxifrage, that snowy flowers emboss,
Supplied the seat; and of the mural moss
The velvet footstool rose, where lightly rest,
Her slender feet in Cypripedium drest.
The tufted rush, that bears a silken crown,
The floating feathers of the thistle's down,

In tender hues of rainbow lustre dyed,
The airy texture of her robe supplied,
And wild convolvuli, yet half unblown,
Form'd, with their wreathing buds, her simple zone,
Some wandering tresses of her radiant hair,
Luxuriant floated on the enamour'd air;
The rest were by the Scandix' points confin'd
And graced a shining knot, her head behind
While, as a sceptre of supreme command,
She waved the Anthoxanthum in her hand.
Around the goddess, as the flies that play,
In countless myriads in the western ray,
The sylphs innumerous throng; whose magic powers
Guard the soft buds, and nurse the infant flowers;

Round the sustaining stems weak tendrils bind,
And save the pollen from dispersing wind;
From suns too ardent, shade their transient hues,
And catch in odorous cups translucent dews.
The ruder tasks of others are, to chase
From vegetable life the insect race,
Break the polluting thread the spider weaves,

And brush the aphis from th' unfolding leaves.
For conquest arm'd these pigmy warriors wield
The thorny lance, and spread the hollow shield
Of lichen tough; or bear, as silver bright,
Lunaria's pearly circlet, firm and light.
On the helm'd head the crimson foxglove glows,
Or Scutellaria guards the martial brows,

While the Leontodon its plumage rears,
And o'er the casque in waving grace appears;
With stern undaunted eye, one warlike chief
Grasps the tall club from Arum's blood-dropt leaf;
This, with the Burdock's hooks annoys his foes,
The purple thorn that borrows from the Rose.
In honeyed nectaries couched, some drive away
The forked insidious earwig from his prey;
Fearless the scaled libellula assail,
Dart their keen lances at the encroaching snail;
Arrest the winged ant, on pinions light,
And strike the headlong beetle in his flight.
Nor less assiduous round their lovely queen,
The lighter forms of female fays are seen;

Rich was the purple vest Floscella wore,
Spun of the tufts the Tradescantia bore;
The Cistus' flowers minute her temple graced,
And threads of Yucca bound her slender waist.
From the wild bee, whose wond'rous labour weaves,
In artful folds the rose's fragrant leaves,
Was borrow'd fair Petalla's light cymar;
And the Hypericum, with spangling star,
O'er her fair locks its bloom minute enwreath'd;
Then, while voluptuous odours round her breath'd,
Came Nectarynia; as the arrowy rays
Of lambent fire round pictur'd seraphs blaze,
So did the Passiflora's radii shed,
Cerulean glory o'er the sylphid's head,

While round her form, the pliant tendrils twined,
And clasp'd the scarf that floated on the wind.
More grave the para-nymph Calyxa drest;
A brown transparent spatha formed her vest;
The silver scales that bound her raven hair,
Xeranthemum's unfading calyx bear;
And a light sash of spiral Ophrys press'd
Her filmy tunic, on her tender breast.
But where shall images or words be found
To paint the fair ethereal forms, that round
The queen of flowers attended ? and the while
Bask'd in her eyes and wanton'd in her smile.

Now towards the earth the gay procession bends,

Lo ! from the buoyant air, the car descends;
Anticipating then the various year,
Flowers of all hues and every month appear,
From every swelling bulb its blossoms rise;
Here, blow the Hyacinths of loveliest dyes,
Breathing of heaven; and there, her royal brows
Begemmed with pearl, the Crown imperial shews;
Peeps the blue Gentian, from the soft'ning ground,
Jonquils and Violets, shed their odours round;
The Honeysuckle rears his scallop'd horn;
A snow of blossoms whiten on the thorn.
Here, like the fatal fruit to Paris given,
That spread fell feuds throughout the fabled heaven,

The yellow Rose her golden globe displays;
There lovelier still, among the spiny sprays
Her blushing rivals glow with brighter dyes,
Than paints the summer sun on western skies.
And the scarce tinged, and paler Rose unveil
Their modest beauties to the sighing gale.
Thro' the deep woodland's wild uncultur'd scene,
Spreads the soft influence of the floral queen;
See a fair pyramid the Chesnut rear,
Its crimson tassels on the Larch appear;
The Fir, dark native of the sullen North,
Owns her soft sway; and slowly springing forth
On the rough Oak are buds minute unfurl'd,
Whose giant produce may command the world !
Each forest thicket feels the balmy air,
And plants that love the shade are blowing there.

Rude rocks with Filices and Bryums smile,
And wastes are gay with Thyme and Chamomile.
Ah ! yet prolong the dear delicious dream,
And trace her power along the mountain stream.
See ! from its rude and rocky source, o'erhung
With female fern, and glossy adder's-tongue
Slowly it wells, in pure and chrystal drops,
And steals soft-gliding, thro' the upland copse;
Then murmuring on, along the willowy sides,
The reed-bird whispers, and the Halcyon hides;
While among sallows pale, and birchen bowers,
Embarks in Fancy's eye the queen of flowers.
O'er her light skiff, of woven bull-rush made,
The Water lily lends a polish'd shade;

While Galium there, of pale and silver hue,
And Epilobiums on the banks that grew,
Form her soft couch; and as the Sylphs divide,
With pliant arms, the still increasing tide,
A thousand leaves along the stream unfold;
Amid its waving swords, in flaming gold

The Iris towers; and here the Arrowhead
And water Crowfoot, more profusely spread
Spangle the quiet current; higher there,
As conscious of her claims, in beauty rare,
Her rosy umbels rears the flow'ring Rush,
While with reflected charms the waters blush.
The naiad now, the year's fair goddess leads,
Through richer pastures and more level meads
Down to the sea; where even the briny sands
Their product offer to her glowing hands;

For there, by sea-dews nurs'd and airs marine,
The Chelidonium blows; in glaucous green,
Each refluent tide the thorn'd Eryngium laves,
And its pale leaves seem tinctured by the waves;
And half-way up the cliff, whose rugged brow
Hangs o'er the ever toiling surge below,
Springs the light Tamarisk.The summit bare,
Is tufted by the Statice; and there,
Crush'd by the fisher, as he stands to mark
Some distant signal or approaching bark,
The Saltwort's starry stalks are thickly sown,
Like humble worth, unheeded and unknown!
From depths where corals spring from chrystal caves,
And break with scarlet branch, the eddying waves,

Where Algæ stream, as change the flowing tides,
And where, half flower, half fish, the Polyp hides,
And long tenacious bands of sea-lace twine
Round palm-shaped leaves impearl'd with coralline.
Enamour'd Fancy now the sea-maids calls,
And from their grottos dim, and shell-paved halls,
Charm'd by her voice, the shining train emerge,
And buoyant float above the circling surge;
Green Byssus, waving in the sea-born gales,
Form'd their thin mantles, and transparent veils,
Panier'd in shells, or bound with silver strings,
Of silken pinna; each her trophy brings
Of plants, from rocks and caverns submarine,
With leathery branch, and bladder'd buds between;
There, its dark folds the pucker'd laver spread,
With trees in miniature of various red;

There flag-shaped olive-leaves, depending hung,
And fairy fans from glossy pebbles sprung;
Then her terrestrial train the nereids meet,
And lay their spoils saline at Flora's feet.
O ! fairest of the fabled forms ! that stream,
Dress'd by wild Fancy, thro' the poet's dream,
Still may thy attributes of leaves and flowers,
Thy garden's rich, and shrub-o'ershadow'd bowers,
And yellow meads, with Spring's first honours bright,

The child's gay heart, and frolic step invite;
And, while the careless wanderer explores,
The umbrageous forest, or the rugged shores,
Climbs the green down, or roams the broom-clad waste,
May Truth, and Nature, form his future taste !
Goddess ! on youth's bless'd hours thy gifts bestow;
Bind the fair wreath on virgin-beauty's brow,

And still may Fancy's brightest flowers be wove
Round the gold chains of hymeneal love.
But most for those, by Sorrow's hands oppress'd,
May thy beds blossom, and thy wilds be dress'd;
And where by Fortune and the world forgot,
The mourner droops in some sequester'd spot,
('Sad luxury to vulgar minds unknown,')
O'er blighted happiness for ever gone,
Yet the dear image seeks not to forget,
But woos his grief, and cherishes regret;
Loving, with fond and lingering pain, to mourn
O'er joys and hopes that never will return;
Thou, visionary power ! mayst bid him view
Forms not less lovely, and as transient too;
And while they soothe the wearied pilgrim's eyes,
Afford an antepast of Paradise.

Fragment
Descriptive of the miseries of War; from a Poem
called 'The Emigrants,' printed in 1793.

To a wild mountain, whose bare summit hides
Its broken eminence in clouds; whose steeps

Are dark with woods: where the receding rocks
Are worn with torrents of dissolving snow;
A wretched woman, pale and breathless, flies,
And, gazing round her, listens to the sound
Of hostile footsteps: No! they die away
Nor noise remains, but of the cataract,
Or surly breeze of night, that mutters low
Among the thickets, where she trembling seeks
A temporary shelter. Clasping close
To her quick throbbing heart her sleeping child,
All she could rescue of the innocent group
That yesterday surrounded her. Escaped
Almost by miracle! Fear, frantic Fear,
Wing'd her weak feet; yet, half repenting now
Her headlong haste, she wishes she had staid
To die with those affrighted Fancy paints
The lawless soldiers' victims. Hark! again
The driving tempest bears the cry of Death;
And with deep, sudden thunder, the dread sound

Of cannon vibrates on the tremulous earth;
While, bursting in the air, the murderous bomb
Glares o'er her mansion. Where the splinters fall
Like scatter'd comets, its destructive path
Is mark'd by wreaths of flame! Then, overwhelm'd
Beneath accumulated horror, sinks
The desolate mourner!
The feudal chief, whose gothic battlements
Frown on the plain beneath, returning home
From distant lands, alone, and in disguise,
Gains at the fall of night his castle walls,
But, at the silent gate no porter sits
To wait his lord's admittance! In the courts
All is drear stillness! Guessing but too well
The fatal truth, he shudders as he goes
Through the mute hall; where, by the blunted light
That the dim moon through painted casement lends,
He sees that devastation has been there;
Then, while each hideous image to his mind
Rises terrific, o'er a bleeding corse
Stumbling he falls; another intercepts

His staggering feet. All, all who used to
With joy to meet him, all his family
Lie murder'd in his way! And the day dawns
On a wild raving maniac, whom a fate
So sudden and calamitous has robb'd
Of reason; and who round his vacant walls
Screams unregarded, and reproaches Heaven!

Hope
Parody on Lord Strangford's 'Just like Love.'
Just like Hope is yonder bow,
That from the centre bends so low,
Where bright prismatic colours shew
How gems of heavenly radiance glow,
Just like Hope!
Yet if, to the illusion new,
The pilgrim should the arch pursue,
Farther and farther from his view,
It flies; then melts in chilling dew,
Just like Hope!

Ye fade, ethereal hues ! for ever,
While, cold Reason, thy endeavour
Sooths not that sad heart, which never
Glows with Hope.

Huge Vapours Brood Above The Clifted Shore

Huge vapours brood above the clifted shore,
Night o'er the ocean settles, dark and mute,
Save where is heard the repercussive roar
Of drowsy billows, on the rugged foot
Of rocks remote; or still more distant tone
Of seamen, in the anchored bark, that tell
The watch relieved; or one deep voice alone,
Singing the hour, and bidding "strike the bell."
All is black shadow, but the lucid line
Marked by the light surf on the level sand,
Or where afar, the ship-lights faintly shine
Like wandering fairy fires, that oft on land
Mislead the pilgrim; such the dubious ray
That wavering reason lends, in life's long darkling way.

Inscription

On a Stone, in the Church-Yard at Boreham, in
Essex; raised by the Honourable Elizabeth Olmius,
to the memory of Ann Gardner, who died at New
Hall, after a faithful Service of Forty Years.

Whate'er of praise, and of regret attend
The grateful servant, and the humble friend,
Where strict integrity and worth unite
To raise the lowly in their Maker's sight,

Are her's; whose faithful service, long approved,
Wept by the mistress whom through life she loved.
Here ends her earthly task; in joyful trust
To share the eternal triumph of the just.

Love And Folly

Love, who now deals to human hearts,
Such ill thrown, yet resistless darts,
That hapless mortals can't withstand them,
Was once less cruel and perverse,
Nor did he then his shafts disperse,
So much at random.

It happened, that the thoughtless child
Was rambling thro' a flowery wild,
Like idle lad in school vacation;
Where sauntering now, and now at rest,
Stroll'd Folly, who to Love address'd
His conversation.
On trifles he had much to say,
Then laughing he propos'd to play,
And stake against Love's bow his bauble;
The quiver'd gamester smil'd and won,
But testy Folly soon began

To fret and squabble.

Loud and more loud the quarrel grows;
From words the wranglers went to blows,
For Folly's rage is prompt to rise;
Till bleeding Love a martyr stood
A stroke from Folly's weapon rude,
Put out his eyes.
Then wild with anguish, Venus pray'd,
For vengeance on the idiot's head,
And begg'd of cloud-compelling Jove,
His swiftest lightening, to destroy,
The mischievous malignant boy
That blinded Love.

'Folly is immortal,' Jove replied,
'But, tho' your prayer must be denied,
'An endless penance is decreed him;
'For Love, tho' blind, will reign around
'The world; but still where-ever found,
'Folly shall lead him.'

Occasional Address
Written for the benefit of a distressed Player, detained
at Brighthelmstone for Debt, November 1792.

When in a thousand swarms, the summer o'er,
The birds of passage quit our English shore,
By various routs the feather'd myriad moves;
The Becca-Fica seeks Italian groves,

No more a Wheat-ear; while the soaring files
Of sea-fowl gather round the Hebrid isles.
But if by bird-lime touch'd, unplumed, confined,
Some poor ill-fated straggler stays behind,
Driven from his transient perch, beneath your eaves
On his unshelter'd head the tempest raves,
While drooping round, redoubling every pain,
His mate and nestlings ask his help in vain.
So we, the buskin and the sock who wear,
And 'strut and fret,' our little season here,
Dismiss'd at length, as fortune bids divide
Some (lucky rogues!) sit down on Thames's side;
Others to Liffy's western banks proceed,
And some, driven far a-field, across the Tweed:
But, pinion'd here, alas! I cannot fly:
The hapless, unplumed, lingering straggler I!
Unless the healing pity you bestow,
Shall imp my shatter'd wings, and let me go.
Hard is his fate, whom evil stars have led
To seek in scenic art precarious bread,

While still, through wild vicissitudes afloat,
A hero now, and now a Sans Culotte!
That eleemosynary bread he gains
Mingling, with real distresses, mimic pains.
See in our group, a pale, lank Falstaff stare!
Much needs he stuffing: while young Ammon there
Rehearses, in a garret, ten feet square!
And as his soft Statira sighs consent,
Roxana comes not but a dun for rent!
Here shiv'ring Edgar, in his blanket roll'd,
Exclaims with too much reason, 'Tom's a-cold! '
And vainly tries his sorrows to divert,
While Goneril or Regan, wash his shirt!
Lo! fresh from Calais, Edward, mighty king!
Revolves, a mutton chop upon a string!
And Hotspur, plucking 'honour from the moon,'
Feeds a sick infant with a pewter spoon!
More bless'd the fisher, who undaunted braves
In his small bark, the impetuous winds and waves;
For though he plough the sea when others sleep,
He draws, like Glendower, spirits from the deep.

And while the storm howls round, amidst his trouble,
Bright moonshine still illuminates the cobble.
Pale with her fears for him, some fair Poissarde ,
Watches his nearing boat; with fond regard
Smiles when she sees his little canvass handing,
And clasps her dripping lover on his landing.
More bless'd the peasant , who, with nervous toil
Hews the rough oak, or breaks the stubborn soil:
Weary, indeed, he sees the evening come,
But then, the rude, yet tranquil hut, his home,
Receives its rustic inmate; then are his,
Secure repose, and dear domestic bliss.
The orchard's blushing fruit, the garden's store,
The pendant hop, that mantles round the door,
Are his: and while cheerful faggots burn,
'His lisping children hail their site's return.'
But wandering Players, 'unhousel'd, unanneal'd,'
And unappointed, scour life's common field,
A flying squadron! disappointments cross 'em,
And the campaign concludes, perhaps, at Horsham.
Oh! ye, whose timely bounty deigns to shed
Compassion's balm upon my luckless head,
Benevolence, with warm and glowing breast,
And soft, celestial mercy, doubly bless'd!
Smile on the generous act! where means are given,
To aid the wretched is to merit heaven.

On The Aphorism

'L'Amitié est l'Amour sans ailes.'

Friendship, as some sage poet sings,
Is chasten'd Love, depriv'd of wings,
Without all wish or power to wander;
Less volatile, but not less tender:
Yet says the proverbs'Sly and slow
'Love creeps, even where he cannot go;'
To clip his pinions then is vain,
His old propensities remain;

And she, who years beyond fifteen,
Has counted twenty, may have seen
How rarely unplum'd Love will stay;
He flies notbut he coolly walks away.

Saint Monica

Among deep woods is the dismantled scite
Of an old Abbey, where the chaunted rite,
By twice ten brethren of the monkish cowl,
Was duly sung; and requiems for the soul
Of the first founder: For the lordly chief,
Who flourish'd paramount of many a fief,
Left here a stipend yearly paid, that they,
The pious monks, for his repose might say
Mass and orisons to Saint Monica.

Beneath the falling archway overgrown
With briars, a bench remains, a single stone,
Where sat the indigent, to wait the dole
Given at the buttery; that the baron's soul
The poor might intercede for; there would rest,
Known by his hat of straw with cockles drest,
And staff and humble weed of watchet gray,
The wandering pilgrim; who came there to pray
The intercession of Saint Monica.
Stern Reformation and the lapse of years
Have reft the windows, and no more appears
Abbot or martyr on the glass anneal'd;
And half the falling cloisters are conceal'd

By ash and elder: the refectory wall
Oft in the storm of night is heard to fall,
When, wearied by the labours of the day,
The half awaken'd cotters, starting say,
'It is the ruins of Saint Monica.'
Now with approaching rain is heard the rill,
Just trickling thro' a deep and hollow gill
By osiers, and the alder's crowding bush,
Reeds, and dwarf elder, and the pithy rush,
Choak'd and impeded: to the lower ground

Slowly it creeps; there traces still are found
Of hollow squares, embank'd with beaten clay,
Where brightly glitter'd in the eye of day
The peopled waters of Saint Monica.

The chapel pavement, where the name and date,
Or monkish rhyme, had mark'd the graven plate,
With docks and nettles now is overgrown;
And brambles trail above the dead unknown.
Impatient of the heat, the straggling ewe
Tinkles her drowsy bell, as nibbling slow
She picks the grass among the thistles gray,
Whose feather'd seed the light air bears away,
O'er the pale relicks of Saint Monica.
Reecho'd by the walls, the owl obscene
Hoots to the night; as thro' the ivy green
Whose matted tods the arch and buttress bind,
Sobs in low gusts the melancholy wind:

The Conium there, her stalks bedropp'd with red,
Rears, with Circea, neighbour of the dead;
Atropa too, that, as the beldams say,
Shews her black fruit to tempt and to betray,
Nods by the mouldering shrine of Monica.
Old tales and legends are not quite forgot.
Still Superstition hovers o'er the spot,
And tells how here, the wan and restless sprite,
By some way-wilder'd peasant seen at night,
Gibbers and shrieks, among the ruins drear;
And how the friar's lanthorn will appear
Gleaming among the woods, with fearful ray,
And from the church-yard take its wavering way,
To the dim arches of Saint Monica.

The antiquary comes not to explore,
As once, the unrafter'd roof and pathless floor;
For now, no more beneath the vaulted ground
Is crosier, cross, or sculptur'd chalice found,
Nor record telling of the wassail ale,
What time the welcome summons to regale,
Given by the matin peal on holiday,
The villagers rejoicing to obey,
Feasted, in honour of Saint Monica.
Yet often still at eve, or early morn,
Among these ruins shagg'd with fern and thorn,
A pensive stranger from his lonely seat
Observes the rapid martin, threading fleet

The broken arch: or follows with his eye,
The wall-creeper that hunts the burnish'd fly;
Sees the newt basking in the sunny ray,
Or snail that sinuous winds his shining way,

O'er the time-fretted walls of Monica.
He comes not here, from the sepulchral stone
To tear the oblivious pall that Time has thrown,
But meditating, marks the power proceed
From the mapped lichen, to the plumed weed,
From thready mosses to the veined flower,
The silent, slow, but ever active power
Of Vegetative Life, that o'er Decay
Weaves her green mantle, when returning May
Dresses the ruins of Saint Monica.

Oh Nature ! ever lovely, ever new,
He whom his earliest vows has paid to you
Still finds, that life has something to bestow;
And while to dark Forgetfulness they go,
Man, and the works of man; immortal Youth,
Unfading Beauty, and eternal Truth,
Your Heaven-indited volume will display,
While Art's elaborate monuments decay,
Even as these shatter'd aisles, deserted Monica !

Studies By The Sea

Ah! wherefore do the incurious say,
That this stupendous ocean wide,
No change presents from day to day,
Save only the alternate tide;
Or save when gales of summer glide
Across the lightly crisped wave;
Or, when against the cliff's rough side,
As equinoctial tempests rave,
It wildly bursts; o'erwhelms the deluged strand,
Tears down its bounds, and desolates the land ?

He who with more enquiring eyes
Doth this extensive scene survey,
Beholds innumerous changes rise,
As various winds its surface sway;
Now o'er its heaving bosom play
Small sparkling waves of silver gleam,
And as they lightly glide away
Illume with fluctuating beam
The deepening surge; green as the dewy corn
That undulates in April's breezy morn.
The far off waters then assume
A glowing amethystine shade,
That changing like the peacock's plume
Seems in celestial blue to fade;

Or paler, colder hues of lead,
As lurid vapours float on high,
Along the ruffling billows spread,

While darkly lours the threatening sky;
And the small scatter'd barks with outspread shrouds,
Catch the long gleams, that fall between the clouds.
Then day's bright star with blunted rays
Seems struggling thro' the sea-fog pale,
And doubtful in the heavy haze,
Is dimly seen the nearing sail;
'Till from the land a fresher gale
Disperses the white mist, and clear,
As melts away the gauzy veil,
The sun-reflecting waves appear;

So, brighter genuine virtue seems to rise
From envy's dark invidious calumnies.
What glories on the sun attend,
When the full tides of evening flow,
Where in still changing beauty, blend
With amber light, the opal's glow;
While in the east the diamond bow
Rises in virgin lustre bright,
And from the horizon seems to throw,
A partial line of trembling light
To the hush'd shore; and all the tranquil deep
Beneath the modest moon, is sooth'd to sleep.

Forgotten then, the thundering break
Of waves, that in the tempest rise,
The falling cliff, the shatter'd wreck,
The howling blast, the sufferer's cries;
For soft the breeze of evening sighs,
And murmuring seems in Fancy's ear
To whisper fairy lullabies,
That tributary waters bear
From precipices, dark with piny woods,
And inland rocks, and heathy solitudes.
The vast encircling seas within,
What endless swarms of creatures hide ,
Of burnish'd scale, and spiny fin !
These providential instincts guide,

And bid them know the annual tide,
When, from unfathom'd waves that swell,
Beyond Fuego's stormy side,
They come, to cheer the tribes that dwell
In Boreal climes; and thro' his half year's night
Give to the Lapland savage, food and light.
From cliffs, that pierce the northern sky;
Where eagles rear their sanguine brood,
With long awaiting patient eye,
Baffled by many a sailing cloud,
The Highland native marks the flood,
Till bright the quickening billows roll,

And hosts of sea-birds, clamouring loud,
Track with wild wing the welcome shoal,

Swift o'er the animated current sweep,
And bear their silver captives from the deep.
Sons of the North ! your streamy vales
With no rich sheaves rejoice and sing;
Her flowery robe no fruit conceals,
Tho' sweetly smile your tardy spring;
Yet every mountain, clothed with ling,
Doth from its purple brow survey
Your busy sails, that ceaseless bring
To the broad frith, and sheltering bay,
Riches, by Heaven's parental power supplied,
The harvest of the far embracing tide.

And, where those fractur'd mountains lift
O'er the blue wave their towering crest,
Each salient ledge and hollow cleft
To sea-fowl give a rugged nest.
But with instinctive love is drest
The Eider's downy cradle; where
The mother-bird, her glossy breast
Devotes, and with maternal care,
And plumeless bosom, stems the toiling seas,
That foam round the tempestuous Orcades.
From heights, whence shuddering sense recoils,
And cloud-capped headlands, steep and bare,
Sons of the North ! your venturous toils
Collect your poor and scanty fare.

Urged by imperious Want, you dare
Scale the loose cliff, where Gannets hide,
Or scarce suspended, in the air
Hang perilous; and thus provide
The soft voluptuous couch, which not secures
To Luxury's pamper'd minions, sleep like yours.
Revolving still, the waves that now
Just ripple on the level shore,
Have borne perchance the Indian's prow,
Or half congeal'd, 'mid ice rocks hoar,
Raved to the Walrus' hollow roar;
Or have by currents swift convey'd
To the cold coast of Labrador,
The relics of the tropic shade;

And to the wondering Esquimaux have shown
Leaves of strange shape, and fruits unlike their own.
No more then, let the incurious say,
No change this world of water shows,
But as the tides the moon obey,
Or tempests rave, or calms repose.

Shew them, its bounteous breast bestows
On myriads life; and bid them see
In every wave that circling flows,
Beauty and use, and harmony
Works of the Power Supreme, who poured the flood,
Round the green peopled earth, and call'd it good !

The Bee's Winter Retreat

Go, while the summer suns are bright,
Take at large thy wandering flight,
Go, and load thy tiny feet
With every rich and various sweet;
Cling around the flowering thorn,
Dive in the woodbine's honey'd horn,
Seek the wild rose that shades the dell,
Explore the foxglove's freckled bell;
Or in the heath-flower's fairy cup,
Drink the fragrant spirit up,
But when the meadows shall be mown,
And summer's garlands overblown,
Then come, thou little busy bee,
And let thy homestead be with me:-
There, shelter'd by the straw-built hive,
In my garden thou shalt live,
And that garden shall supply
Thy delicious alchymy;-
There, for thee, in autumn, blows
The Indian pink and latest rose,
The mignonette perfumes the air,
And stocks, unfading flowers, are there.

Yet fear not when the tempests come,
And drive thee to thy waxen home,
That I shall then, most treacherously,
For thy honey murder thee:-
Oh, no! -throughout the winter drear
I'll feed thee, that another year
Thou may'st renew thy industry
Among the flowers, thou busy bee.

The Dead Beggar

An Elegy.
Addressed to a Lady, who was affected at seeing the funeral of a nameless
Pauper, buried at the expense of the Parish, in the Church-Yard at
Brighthelmstone, in November 1792.

Swells then thy feeling heart, and streams thine eye
O'er the deserted being, poor and old,
Whom cold, reluctant, parish charity
Consigns to mingle with his kindred mould?

Mourn'st thou, that here the time-worn sufferer ends
Those evil days still threatening woes to come;
Here, where the friendless feel no want of friends,
Where even the houseless wanderer finds a home!

What though no kindred crowd in sable forth,
And sigh, or seem to sigh, around his bier;
Though o'er his coffin with the humid earth
No children drop the unavailing tear?
Rather rejoice that here his sorrows cease,
Whom sickness, age, and poverty oppress'd;
Where death, the leveller, restores to peace
The wretch who living knew not where to rest.
Rejoice, that though an outcast spurn'd by fate,
Through penury's rugged path his race he ran;
In earth's cold bosom, equall'd with the great,
Death vindicates the insulted rights of man.
Rejoice, that though severe his earthly doom,
And rude, and sown with thorns the way he trod,
Now, (where unfeeling fortune cannot come)
He rests upon the mercies of his God.

The Emigrants: Book I
Scene, on the Cliffs to the Eastward of the Town of Brighthelmstone in Sussex.
Time, a Morning in November, 1792.

Slow in the Wintry Morn, the struggling light
Throws a faint gleam upon the troubled waves;
Their foaming tops, as they approach the shore
And the broad surf that never ceasing breaks
On the innumerous pebbles, catch the beams
Of the pale Sun, that with reluctance gives
To this cold northern Isle, its shorten'd day.
Alas! how few the morning wakes to joy!
How many murmur at oblivious night
For leaving them so soon; for bearing thus
Their fancied bliss (the only bliss they taste!),
On her black wings away! Changing the dreams
That sooth'd their sorrows, for calamities
(And every day brings its own sad proportion)
For doubts, diseases, abject dread of Death,
And faithless friends, and fame and fortune lost;
Fancied or real wants; and wounded pride,
That views the day star, but to curse his beams.
Yet He, whose Spirit into being call'd
This wond'rous World of Waters; He who bids
The wild wind lift them till they dash the clouds,
And speaks to them in thunder; or whose breath,
Low murmuring, o'er the gently heaving tides,
When the fair Moon, in summer night serene,
Irradiates with long trembling lines of light

Their undulating surface; that great Power,
Who, governing the Planets, also knows
If but a Sea-Mew falls, whose nest is hid
In these incumbent cliffs; He surely means
To us, his reasoning Creatures, whom He bids
Acknowledge and revere his awful hand,
Nothing but good: Yet Man, misguided Man,
Mars the fair work that he was bid enjoy,
And makes himself the evil he deplores.
How often, when my weary soul recoils
From proud oppression, and from legal crimes
(For such are in this Land, where the vain boast
Of equal Law is mockery, while the cost
Of seeking for redress is sure to plunge
Th' already injur'd to more certain ruin
And the wretch starves, before his Counsel pleads)
How often do I half abjure Society,
And sigh for some lone Cottage, deep embower'd
In the green woods, that these steep chalky Hills
Guard from the strong South West; where round their base
The Beach wide flourishes, and the light Ash
With slender leaf half hides the thymy turf!
There do I wish to hide me; well content
If on the short grass, strewn with fairy flowers,
I might repose thus shelter'd; or when Eve
In Orient crimson lingers in the west,
Gain the high mound, and mark these waves remote
(Lucid tho' distant), blushing with the rays
Of the far-flaming Orb, that sinks beneath them;
For I have thought, that I should then behold
The beauteous works of God, unspoil'd by Man
And less affected then, by human woes
I witness'd not; might better learn to bear
Those that injustice, and duplicity
And faithlessness and folly, fix on me:
For never yet could I derive relief,
When my swol'n heart was bursting with its sorrows,
From the sad thought, that others like myself
Live but to swell affliction's countless tribes!
Tranquil seclusion I have vainly sought;
Peace, who delights solitary shade,
No more will spread for me her downy wings,
But, like the fabled Danaïds or the wretch,
Who ceaseless, up the steep acclivity,
Was doom'd to heave the still rebounding rock,
Onward I labour; as the baffled wave,
Which yon rough beach repulses, that returns
With the next breath of wind, to fail again.
Ah! Mourner cease these wailings: cease and learn,
That not the Cot sequester'd, where the briar
And wood-bine wild, embrace the mossy thatch,
(Scarce seen amid the forest gloom obscure!)

Or more substantial farm, well fenced and warm,
Where the full barn, and cattle fodder'd round
Speak rustic plenty; nor the statelier dome
By dark firs shaded, or the aspiring pine,
Close by the village Church (with care conceal'd
By verdant foliage, lest the poor man's grave
Should mar the smiling prospect of his Lord),
Where offices well rang'd, or dove-cote stock'd,
Declare manorial residence; not these
Or any of the buildings, new and trim
With windows circling towards the restless Sea,
Which ranged in rows, now terminate my walk,
Can shut out for an hour the spectre Care,
That from the dawn of reason, follows still
Unhappy Mortals, 'till the friendly grave
(Our sole secure asylum) "ends the chace."
Behold, in witness of this mournful truth,
A group approach me, whose dejected looks,
Sad Heralds of distress! proclaim them Men
Banish'd for ever and for conscience sake
From their distracted Country, whence the name
Of Freedom misapplied, and much abus'd
By lawless Anarchy, has driven them far
To wander; with the prejudice they learn'd
From Bigotry (the Tut'ress of the blind),
Thro' the wide World unshelter'd; their sole hope,
That German spoilers, thro' that pleasant land
May carry wide the desolating scourge
Of War and Vengeance; yet unhappy Men,
Whate'er your errors, I lament your fate:
And, as disconsolate and sad ye hang
Upon the barrier of the rock, and seem
To murmur your despondence, waiting long
Some fortunate reverse that never comes;
Methinks in each expressive face, I see
Discriminated anguish; there droops one,
Who in a moping cloister long consum'd
This life inactive, to obtain a better,
And thought that meagre abstinence, to wake
From his hard pallet with the midnight bell,
To live on eleemosynary bread,
And to renounce God's works, would please that God.
And now the poor pale wretch receives, amaz'd,
The pity, strangers give to his distress,
Because these Strangers are, by his dark creed,
Condemn'd as Heretics and with sick heart
Regrets his pious prison, and his beads.
Another, of more haughty port, declines
The aid he needs not; while in mute despair
His high indignant thoughts go back to France,
Dwelling on all he lost, the Gothic dome,
That vied with splendid palaces; the beds

Of silk and down, the silver chalices,
Vestments with gold enwrought for blazing altars;
Where, amid clouds of incense, he held forth
To kneeling crowds the imaginary bones
Of Saints suppos'd, in pearl and gold enchas'd,
And still with more than living Monarchs' pomp
Surrounded; was believ'd by mumbling bigots
To hold the keys of Heaven, and to admit
Whom he thought good to share it. Now alas!
He, to whose daring soul and high ambition
The World seem'd circumscrib'd; who, wont to dream,
Of Fleuri, Richelieu, Alberoni, men
Who trod on Empire, and whose politics
Were not beyond the grasp of his vast mind,
Is, in a Land once hostile, still prophan'd
By disbelief, and rites un-orthodox,
The object of compassion. At his side,
Lighter of heart than these, but heavier far
Than he was wont, another victim comes,
An Abbé who with less contracted brow
Still smiles and flatters, and still talks of Hope;
Which, sanguine as he is, he does not feel,
And so he cheats the sad and weighty pressure
Of evils present; Still, as Men misled
By early prejudice (so hard to break),
I mourn your sorrows; for I too have known
Involuntary exile; and while yet
England had charms for me, have felt how sad
It is to look across the dim cold sea,
That melancholy rolls its refluent tides
Between us and the dear regretted land
We call our own as now ye pensive wait
On this bleak morning, gazing on the waves
That seem to leave your shore; from whence the wind
Is loaded to your ears, with the deep groans
Of martyr'd Saints and suffering Royalty,
While to your eyes the avenging power of Heaven
Appears in aweful anger to prepare
The storm of vengeance, fraught with plagues and death.
Even he of milder heart, who was indeed
The simple shepherd in a rustic scene,
And, 'mid the vine-clad hills of Languedoc,
Taught to the bare-foot peasant, whose hard hands
Produc'd the nectar he could seldom taste,
Submission to the Lord for whom he toil'd;
He, or his brethren, who to Neustria's sons
Enforc'd religious patience, when, at times,
On their indignant hearts Power's iron hand
Too strongly struck; eliciting some sparks
Of the bold spirit of their native North;
Even these Parochial Priests, these humbled men;
Whose lowly undistinguish'd cottages

Witness'd a life of purest piety,
While the meek tenants were, perhaps, unknown
Each to the haughty Lord of his domain,
Who mark'd them not; the Noble scorning still
The poor and pious Priest, as with slow pace
He glided thro' the dim arch'd avenue
Which to the Castle led; hoping to cheer
The last sad hour of some laborious life
That hasten'd to its close even such a Man
Becomes an exile; staying not to try
By temperate zeal to check his madd'ning flock,
Who, at the novel sound of Liberty
(Ah! most intoxicating sound to slaves!),
Start into licence. Lo! dejected now,
The wandering Pastor mourns, with bleeding heart,
His erring people, weeps and prays for them,
And trembles for the account that he must give
To Heaven for souls entrusted to his care.
Where the cliff, hollow'd by the wintry storm,
Affords a seat with matted sea-weed strewn,
A softer form reclines; around her run,
On the rough shingles, or the chalky bourn,
Her gay unconscious children, soon amus'd;
Who pick the fretted stone, or glossy shell,
Or crimson plant marine: or they contrive
The fairy vessel, with its ribband sail
And gilded paper pennant: in the pool,
Left by the salt wave on the yielding sands,
They launch the mimic navy. Happy age!
Unmindful of the miseries of Man!
Alas! too long a victim to distress,
Their Mother, lost in melancholy thought,
Lull'd for a moment by the murmurs low
Of sullen billows, wearied by the task
Of having here, with swol'n and aching eyes
Fix'd on the grey horizon, since the dawn
Solicitously watch'd the weekly sail
From her dear native land, now yields awhile
To kind forgetfulness, while Fancy brings,
In waking dreams, that native land again!
Versailles appears its painted galleries,
And rooms of regal splendour, rich with gold,
Where, by long mirrors multiply'd, the crowd
Paid willing homage and, united there,
Beauty gave charms to empire. Ah! too soon
From the gay visionary pageant rous'd,
See the sad mourner start! and, drooping, look
With tearful eyes and heaving bosom round
On drear reality where dark'ning waves,
Urg'd by the rising wind, unheeded foam
Near her cold rugged seat: To call her thence
A fellow-sufferer comes: dejection deep

Checks, but conceals not quite, the martial air,
And that high consciousness of noble blood,
Which he has learn'd from infancy to think
Exalts him o'er the race of common men:
Nurs'd in the velvet lap of luxury,
And fed by adulation could he learn,
That worth alone is true Nobility?
And that the peasant who, "amid the sons
"Of Reason, Valour, Liberty, and Virtue,
"Displays distinguish'd merit, is a Noble
"Of Nature's own creation!" If even here,
If in this land of highly vaunted Freedom,
Even Britons controvert the unwelcome truth,
Can it be relish'd by the sons of France?
Men, who derive their boasted ancestry
From the fierce leaders of religious wars,
The first in Chivalry's emblazon'd page;
Who reckon Gueslin, Bayard, or De Foix,
Among their brave Progenitors? Their eyes,
Accustom'd to regard the splendid trophies
Of Heraldry (that with fantastic hand
Mingles, like images in feverish dreams,
"Gorgons and Hydras, and Chimeras dire,"
With painted puns, and visionary shapes;),
See not the simple dignity of Virtue,
But hold all base, whom honours such as these
Exalt not from the crowd. As one, who long
Has dwelt amid the artificial scenes
Of populous City, deems that splendid shows,
The Theatre, and pageant pomp of Courts,
Are only worth regard; forgets all taste
For Nature's genuine beauty; in the lapse
Of gushing waters hears no soothing sound,
Nor listens with delight to sighing winds,
That, on their fragrant pinions, waft the notes
Of birds rejoicing in the trangled copse;
Nor gazes pleas'd on Ocean's silver breast,
While lightly o'er it sails the summer clouds
Reflected in the wave, that, hardly heard,
Flows on the yellow sands: so to his mind,
That long has liv'd where Despotism hides
His features harsh, beneath the diadem
Of worldly grandeur, abject Slavery seems,
If by that power impos'd, slavery no more:
For luxury wreathes with silk the iron bonds,
And hides the ugly rivets with her flowers,
Till the degenerate triflers, while they love
The glitter of the chains, forget their weight.
But more the Men, whose ill acquir'd wealth
Was wrung from plunder'd myriads, by the means
Too often legaliz'd by power abus'd,
Feel all the horrors of the fatal change,

When their ephemeral greatness, marr'd at once
(As a vain toy that Fortune's childish hand
Equally joy'd to fashion or to crush),
Leaves them expos'd to universal scorn
For having nothing else; not even the claim
To honour, which respect for Heroes past
Allows to ancient titles; Men, like these,
Sink even beneath the level, whence base arts
Alone had rais'd them; unlamented sink,
And know that they deserve the woes they feel.
Poor wand'ring wretches! whosoe'er ye are,
That hopeless, houseless, friendless, travel wide
O'er these bleak russet downs; where, dimly seen,
The solitary Shepherd shiv'ring tends
His dun discolour'd flock (Shepherd, unlike
Him, whom in song the Poet's fancy crowns
With garlands, and his crook with vi'lets binds);
Poor vagrant wretches! outcasts of the world!
Whom no abode receives, no parish owns;
Roving, like Nature's commoners, the land
That boasts such general plenty: if the sight
Of wide-extended misery softens yours
Awhile, suspend your murmurs! here behold
The strange vicissitudes of fate, while thus
The exil'd Nobles, from their country driven,
Whose richest luxuries were their's, must feel
More poignant anguish, than the lowest poor,
Who, born to indigence, have learn'd to brave
Rigid Adversity's depressing breath!
Ah! rather Fortune's worthless favourites!
Who feed on England's vitals. Pensioners
Of base corruption, who, in quick ascent
To opulence unmerited, become
Giddy with pride, and as ye rise, forgetting
The dust ye lately left, with scorn look down
On those beneath ye (tho' your equals once
In fortune , and in worth superior still ,
They view the eminence, on which ye stand,
With wonder, not with envy; for they know
The means, by which ye reach'd it, have been such
As, in all honest eyes, degrade ye far
Beneath the poor dependent, whose sad heart
Reluctant pleads for what your pride denies);
Ye venal, worthless hirelings of a Court!
Ye pamper'd Parasites! whom Britons pay
For forging fetters for them; rather here
Study a lesson that concerns ye much;
And, trembling, learn, that if oppress'd too long,
The raging multitude, to madness stung,
Will turn on their oppressors; and, no more
By sounding titles and parading forms
Bound like tame victims, will redress themselves!

Then swept away by the resistless torrent,
Not only all your pomp may disappear,
But, in the tempest lost, fair Order sink
Her decent head, and lawless Anarchy
O'erturn celestial Freedom's radiant throne;
As now in Gallia; where Confusion, born
Of party rage and selfish love of rule,
Sully the noblest cause that ever warm'd
The heart of Patriot Virtue. There arise
The infernal passions; Vengeance, seeking blood,
And Avarice; and Envy's harpy fangs
Pollute the immortal shrine of Liberty,
Dismay her votaries, and disgrace her name.
Respect is due to principle; and they,
Who suffer for their conscience, have a claim,
Whate'er that principle may be, to praise.
These ill-starr'd Exiles then, who, bound by ties,
To them the bonds of honour; who resign'd
Their country to preserve them, and now seek
In England an asylum well deserve
To find that (every prejudice forgot,
Which pride and ignorance teaches), we for them
Feel as our brethren; and that English hearts,
Of just compassion ever own the sway,
As truly as our element, the deep,
Obeys the mild dominion of the Moon
This they have found; and may they find it still!
Thus may'st thou, Britain, triumph! May thy foes,
By Reason's gen'rous potency subdued,
Learn, that the God thou worshippest, delights
In acts of pure humanity! May thine
Be still such bloodless laurels! nobler far
Than those acquir'd at Cressy or Poictiers,
Or of more recent growth, those well bestow'd
On him who stood on Calpe's blazing height
Amid the thunder of a warring world,
Illustrious rather from the crowds he sav'd
From flood and fire, than from the ranks who fell
Beneath his valour! Actions such as these,
Like incense rising to the Throne of Heaven,
Far better justify the pride, that swells
In British bosoms, than the deafening roar
Of Victory from a thousand brazen throats,
That tell with what success wide-wasting War
Has by our brave Compatriots thinned the world.

The Emigrants: Book II

Scene, on an Eminence on one of those Downs, which afford to the South a view of the Sea; to the North of the Weald of Sussex. Time, an Afternoon in April, 1793.

Long wintry months are past; the Moon that now
Lights her pale crescent even at noon, has made
Four times her revolution; since with step,
Mournful and slow, along the wave-worn cliff,
Pensive I took my solitary way,
Lost in despondence, while contemplating
Not my own wayward destiny alone,
(Hard as it is, and difficult to bear!)
But in beholding the unhappy lot
Of the lorn Exiles; who, amid the storms
Of wild disastrous Anarchy, are thrown,
Like shipwreck'd sufferers, on England's coast,
To see, perhaps, no more their native land,
Where Desolation riots: They, like me,
From fairer hopes and happier prospects driven,
Shrink from the future, and regret the past.
But on this Upland scene, while April comes,
With fragrant airs, to fan my throbbing breast,
Fain would I snatch an interval from Care,
That weighs my wearied spirit down to earth;
Courting, once more, the influence of Hope
(For "Hope" still waits upon the flowery prime)
As here I mark Spring's humid hand unfold
The early leaves that fear capricious winds,
While, even on shelter'd banks, the timid flowers
Give, half reluctantly, their warmer hues
To mingle with the primroses' pale stars.
No shade the leafless copses yet afford,
Nor hide the mossy labours of the Thrush,
That, startled, darts across the narrow path;
But quickly re-assur'd, resumes his talk,
Or adds his louder notes to those that rise
From yonder tufted brake; where the white buds
Of the first thorn are mingled with the leaves
Of that which blossoms on the brow of May.
Ah! 'twill not be: So many years have pass'd,
Since, on my native hills, I learn'd to gaze
On these delightful landscapes; and those years
Have taught me so much sorrow, that my soul
Feels not the joy reviving Nature brings;
But, in dark retrospect, dejected dwells
On human follies, and on human woes.
What is the promise of the infant year,
The lively verdure, or the bursting blooms,
To those, who shrink from horrors such as War
Spreads o'er the affrighted world? With swimming eye,
Back on the past they throw their mournful looks,
And see the Temple, which they fondly hop'd
Reason would raise to Liberty, destroy'd
By ruffian hands; while, on the ruin'd mass,
Flush'd with hot blood, the Fiend of Discord sits
In savage triumph; mocking every plea

Of policy and justice, as she shews
The headless corse of one, whose only crime
Was being born a Monarch. Mercy turns,
From spectacle so dire, her swol'n eyes;
And Liberty, with calm, unruffled brow
Magnanimous, as conscious of her strength
In Reason's panoply, scorns to distain
Her righteous cause with carnage, and resigns
To Fraud and Anarchy the infuriate crowd.
What is the promise of the infant year
To those, who (while the poor but peaceful hind
Pens, unmolested, the encreasing flock
Of his rich master in this sea-fenc'd isle)
Survey, in neighbouring countries, scenes that make
The sick heart shudder; and the Man, who thinks,
Blush for his species? There the trumpet's voice
Drowns the soft warbling of the woodland choir;
And violets, lurking in their turfy beds
Beneath the flow'ring thorn, are stain'd with blood.
There fall, at once, the spoiler and the spoil'd;
While War, wide-ravaging, annihilates
The hope of cultivation; gives to Fiends,
The meagre, ghastly Fiends of Want and Woe,
The blasted land. There, taunting in the van
Of vengeance-breathing armies, Insult stalks;
And, in the ranks, " Famine, and Sword, and Fire,
"Crouch for employment." Lo! the suffering world,
Torn by the fearful conflict, shrinks, amaz'd,
From Freedom's name, usurp'd and misapplied,
And, cow'ring to the purple Tyrant's rod,
Deems that the lesser ill. Deluded Men!
Ere ye prophane her ever-glorious name,
Or catalogue the thousands that have bled
Resisting her; or those, who greatly died
Martyrs to Liberty revert awhile
To the black scroll, that tells of regal crimes
Committed to destroy her; rather count
The hecatombs of victims, who have fallen
Beneath a single despot; or who gave
Their wasted lives for some disputed claim
Between anointed robbers: Monsters both!
"Oh! Polish'd perturbation, golden care!"
So strangely coveted by feeble Man
To lift him o'er his fellows; Toy, for which
Such showers of blood have drench'd th' affrighted earth
Unfortunate his lot, whose luckless head
Thy jewel'd circlet, lin'd with thorns, has bound;
And who, by custom's laws, obtains from thee
Hereditary right to rule, uncheck'd,
Submissive myriads: for untemper'd power,
Like steel ill form'd, injures the hand
It promis'd to protect. Unhappy France!

If e'er thy lilies, trampled now in dust,
And blood-bespotted, shall again revive
In silver splendour, may the wreath be wov'n
By voluntary hands; and Freemen, such
As England's self might boast, unite to place
The guarded diadem on his fair brow,
Where Loyalty may join with Liberty
To fix it firmly. In the rugged school
Of stern Adversity so early train'd,
His future life, perchance, may emulate
That of the brave Bernois, so justly call'd
The darling of his people; who rever'd
The Warrior less, than they ador'd the Man!
But ne'er may Party Rage, perverse and blind,
And base Venality, prevail to raise
To public trust, a wretch, whose private vice
Makes even the wildest profligate recoil;
And who, with hireling ruffians leagu'd, has burst
The laws of Nature and Humanity!
Wading, beneath the Patriot's specious mask,
And in Equality's illusive name,
To empire thro' a stream of kindred blood
Innocent prisoner! most unhappy heir
Of fatal greatness, who art suffering now
For all the crimes and follies of thy race;
Better for thee, if o'er thy baby brow
The regal mischief never had been held:
Then, in an humble sphere, perhaps content,
Thou hadst been free and joyous on the heights
Of Pyrennean mountains, shagg'd with woods
Of chesnut, pine, and oak: as on these hills
Is yonder little thoughtless shepherd lad,
Who, on the slope abrupt of downy turf
Reclin'd in playful indolence, sends off
The chalky ball, quick bounding far below;
While, half forgetful of his simple task,
Hardly his length'ning shadow, or the bells'
Slow tinkling of his flock, that supping tend
To the brown fallows in the vale beneath,
Where nightly it is folded, from his sport
Recal the happy idler. While I gaze
On his gay vacant countenance, my thoughts
Compare with his obscure, laborious lot,
Thine, most unfortunate, imperial Boy!
Who round thy sullen prison daily hear'st
The savage howl of Murder, as it seeks
Thy unoffending life: while sad within
Thy wretched Mother, petrified with grief,
Views thee with stony eyes, and cannot weep!
Ah! much I mourn thy sorrows, hapless Queen!
And deem thy expiation made to Heaven
For every fault, to which Prosperity

Betray'd thee, when it plac'd thee on a throne
Where boundless power was thine, and thou wert rais'd
High (as it seem'd) above the envious reach
Of destiny! Whate'er thy errors were,
Be they no more remember'd; tho' the rage
Of Party swell'd them to such crimes, as bade
Compassion stifle every sigh that rose
For thy disastrous lot. More than enough
Thou hast endur'd; and every English heart,
Ev'n those, that highest beat in Freedom's cause,
Disclaim as base, and of that cause unworthy,
The Vengeance, or the Fear, that makes thee still
A miserable prisoner! Ah! who knows,
From sad experience, more than I, to feel
For thy desponding spirit, as it sinks
Beneath procrastinated fears for those
More dear to thee than life! But eminence
Of misery is thine, as once of joy;
And, as we view the strange vicissitude,
We ask anew, where happiness is found?
Alas! in rural life, where youthful dreams
See the Arcadia that Romance describes,
Not even Content resides! In yon low hut
Of clay and thatch, where rises the grey smoke
Of smold'ring turf, cut from the adjoining moor,
The labourer, its inhabitant, who toils
From the first dawn of twilight, till the Sun
Sinks in the rosy waters of the West,
Finds that with poverty it cannot dwell;
For bread, and scanty bread, is all he earns
For him and for his household. Should Disease,
Born of chill wintry rains, arrest his arm,
Then, thro' his patch'd and straw-stuff'd casement, peeps
The squalid figure of extremest Want;
And from the Parish the reluctant dole,
Dealt by th' unfeeling farmer, hardly saves
The ling'ring spark of life from cold extinction:
Then the bright Sun of Spring, that smiling bids
All other animals rejoice, beholds,
Crept from his pallet, the emaciate wretch
Attempt, with feeble effort, to resume
Some heavy task, above his wasted strength,
Turning his wistful looks (how much in vain!)
To the deserted mansion, where no more
The owner (gone to gayer scenes) resides,
Who made even luxury, Virtue; while he gave
The scatter'd crumbs to honest Poverty.
But, tho' the landscape be too oft deform'd
By figures such as these, yet Peace is here,
And o'er our vallies, cloath'd with springing corn,
No hostile hoof shall trample, nor fierce flames
Wither the wood's young verdure, ere it form

Gradual the laughing May's luxuriant shade;
For, by the rude sea guarded, we are safe,
And feel not evils such as with deep sighs
The Emigrants deplore, as, they recal
The Summer past, when Nature seem'd to lose
Her course in wild distemperature, and aid,
With seasons all revers'd, destructive War.
Shuddering, I view the pictures they have drawn
Of desolated countries, where the ground,
Stripp'd of its unripe produce, was thick strewn
With various Death, the war-horse falling there
By famine, and his rider by the sword.
The moping clouds sail'd heavy charg'd with rain,
And bursting o'er the mountains misty brow,
Deluged, as with an inland sea, the vales;
Where, thro' the sullen evening's lurid gloom,
Rising, like columns of volcanic fire,
The flames of burning villages illum'd
The waste of water; and the wind, that howl'd
Along its troubled surface, brought the groans
Of plunder'd peasants, and the frantic shrieks
Of mothers for their children; while the brave,
To pity still alive, listen'd aghast
To these dire echoes, hopeless to prevent
The evils they beheld, or check the rage,
Which ever, as the people of one land
Meet in contention, fires the human heart
With savage thirst of kindred blood, and makes
Man lose his nature; rendering him more fierce
Than the gaunt monsters of the howling waste.
Oft have I heard the melancholy tale,
Which, all their native gaiety forgot,
These Exiles tell. How Hope impell'd them on,
Reckless of tempest, hunger, or the sword,
Till order'd to retreat, they knew not why,
From all their flattering prospects, they became
The prey of dark suspicion and regret:
Then, in despondence, sunk the unnerv'd arm
Of gallant Loyalty. At every turn
Shame and disgrace appear'd, and seem'd to mock
Their scatter'd squadrons; which the warlike youth,
Unable to endure, often implor'd,
As the last act of friendship, from the hand
Of some brave comrade, to receive the blow
That freed the indignant spirit from its pain.
To a wild mountain, whose bare summit hides
Its broken eminence in clouds; whose steeps
Are dark with woods; where the receding rocks
Are worn by torrents of dissolving snow,
A wretched Woman, pale and breathless, flies!
And, gazing round her, listens to the sound
Of hostile footsteps. No! it dies away:

Nor noise remains, but of the cataract,
Or surly breeze of night, that mutters low
Among the thickets, where she trembling seeks
A temporary shelter clasping close
To her hard-heaving heart, her sleeping child,
All she could rescue of the innocent groupe
That yesterday surrounded her. Escap'd
Almost by miracle! Fear, frantic Fear,
Wing'd her weak feet: yet, half repentant now
Her headlong haste, she wishes she had staid
To die with those affrighted Fancy paints
The lawless soldier's victims. Hark! again
The driving tempest bears the cry of Death,
And, with deep sudden thunder, the dread sound
Of cannon vibrates on the tremulous earth;
While, bursting in the air, the murderous bomb
Glares o'er her mansion. Where the splinters fall,
Like scatter'd comets, its destructive path
Is mark'd by wreaths of flame! Then, overwhelm'd
Beneath accumulated horror, sinks
The desolate mourner; yet, in Death itself,
True to maternal tenderness, she tries
To save the unconscious infant from the storm
In which she perishes; and to protect
This last dear object of her ruin'd hopes
From prowling monsters, that from other hills,
More inaccessible, and wilder wastes,
Lur'd by the scent of slaughter, follow fierce
Contending hosts, and to polluted fields
Add dire increase of horrors. But alas!
The Mother and the Infant perish both!
The feudal Chief, whose Gothic battlements
Frown on the plain beneath, returning home
From distant lands, alone and in disguise,
Gains at the fall of night his Castle walls,
But, at the vacant gate, no Porter sits
To wait his Lord's admittance! In the courts
All is drear silence! Guessing but too well
The fatal truth, he shudders as he goes
Thro' the mute hall; where, by the blunted light
That the dim moon thro' painted casements lends,
He sees that devastation has been there:
Then, while each hideous image to his mind
Rises terrific, o'er a bleeding corse
Stumbling he falls; another interrupts
His staggering feet all, all who us'd to rush
With joy to meet him all his family
Lie murder'd in his way! And the day dawns
On a wild raving Maniac, whom a fate
So sudden and calamitous has robb'd
Of reason; and who round his vacant walls
Screams unregarded, and reproaches Heaven!

Such are thy dreadful trophies, savage War!
And evils such as these, or yet more dire,
Which the pain'd mind recoils from, all are thine
The purple Pestilence, that to the grave
Sends whom the sword has spar'd, is thine; and thine
The Widow's anguish and the Orphan's tears!
Woes such as these does Man inflict on Man;
And by the closet murderers, whom we style
Wise Politicians; are the schemes prepar'd,
Which, to keep Europe's wavering balance even,
Depopulate her kingdoms, and consign
To tears and anguish half a bleeding world!
Oh! could the time return, when thoughts like these
Spoil'd not that gay delight, which vernal Suns,
Illuminating hills, and woods, and fields,
Gave to my infant spirits. Memory come!
And from distracting cares, that now deprive
Such scenes of all their beauty, kindly bear
My fancy to those hours of simple joy,
When, on the banks of Arun, which I see
Make its irriguous course thro' yonder meads,
I play'd; unconscious then of future ill!
There (where, from hollows fring'd with yellow broom,
The birch with silver rind, and fairy leaf,
Aslant the low stream trembles) I have stood,
And meditated how to venture best
Into the shallow current, to procure
The willow herb of glowing purple spikes,
Or flags, whose sword-like leaves conceal'd the tide,
Startling the timid reed-bird from her nest,
As with aquatic flowers I wove the wreath,
Such as, collected by the shepherd girls,
Deck in the villages the turfy shrine,
And mark the arrival of propitious May.
How little dream'd I then the time would come,
When the bright Sun of that delicious month
Should, from disturb'd and artificial sleep,
Awaken me to never-ending toil,
To terror and to tears! Attempting still,
With feeble hands and cold desponding heart,
To save my children from the o'erwhelming wrongs,
That have for ten long years been heap'd on me!
The fearful spectres of chicane and fraud
Have, Proteus like, still chang'd their hideous forms
(As the Law lent its plausible disguise),
Pursuing my faint steps; and I have seen
Friendship's sweet bonds (which were so early form'd,)
And once I fondly thought of amaranth
Inwove with silver seven times tried) give way,
And fail; as these green fan-like leaves of fern
Will wither at the touch of Autumn's frost.
Yet there are those , whose patient pity still

Hears my long murmurs; who, unwearied, try
With lenient hands to bind up every wound
My wearied spirit feels, and bid me go
"Right onward" a calm votary of the Nymph,
Who, from her adamantine rock, points out
To conscious rectitude the rugged path,
That leads at length to Peace! Ah! yes, my friends
Peace will at last be mine; for in the Grave
Is Peace and pass a few short years, perchance
A few short months, and all the various pain
I now endure shall be forgotten there,
And no memorial shall remain of me,
Save in your bosoms; while even your regret
Shall lose its poignancy, as ye reflect
What complicated woes that grave conceals!
But, if the little praise, that may await
The Mother's efforts, should provoke the spleen
Of Priest or Levite; and they then arraign
The dust that cannot hear them; be it yours
To vindicate my humble fame; to say,
That, not in selfish sufferings absorb'd,
"I gave to misery all I had, my tears."
And if, where regulated sanctity
Pours her long orisons to Heaven, my voice
Was seldom heard, that yet my prayer was made
To him who hears even silence; not in domes
Of human architecture, fill'd with crowds,
But on these hills, where boundless, yet distinct,
Even as a map, beneath are spread the fields
His bounty cloaths; divided here by woods,
And there by commons rude, or winding brooks,
While I might breathe the air perfum'd with flowers,
Or the fresh odours of the mountain turf;
And gaze on clouds above me, as they sail'd
Majestic: or remark the reddening north,
When bickering arrows of electric fire
Flash on the evening sky. I made my prayer
In unison with murmuring waves that now
Swell with dark tempests, now are mild and blue,
As the bright arch above; for all to me
Declare omniscient goodness; nor need I
Declamatory essays to incite
My wonder or my praise, when every leaf
That Spring unfolds, and every simple bud,
More forcibly impresses on my heart
His power and wisdom. Ah! while I adore
That goodness, which design'd to all that lives
Some taste of happiness, my soul is pain'd
By the variety of woes that Man
For Man creates his blessings often turn'd
To plagues and curses: Saint-like Piety,
Misled by Superstition, has destroy'd

More than Ambition; and the sacred flame
Of Liberty becomes a raging fire,
When Licence and Confusion bid it blaze.
From thy high throne, above yon radiant stars,
O Power Omnipotent! with mercy view
This suffering globe, and cause thy creatures cease,
With savage fangs, to tear her bleeding breast:
Refrain that rage for power, that bids a Man,
Himself a worm, desire unbounded rule
O'er beings like himself: Teach the hard hearts
Of rulers, that the poorest hind, who dies
For their unrighteous quarrels, in thy sight
Is equal to the imperious Lord, that leads
His disciplin'd destroyers to the field.
May lovely Freedom, in her genuine charms,
Aided by stern but equal Justice, drive
From the ensanguin'd earth the hell-born fiends
Of Pride, Oppression, Avarice, and Revenge,
That ruin what thy mercy made so fair!
Then shall these ill-starr'd wanderers, whose sad fate
These desultory lines lament, regain
Their native country; private vengeance then
To public virtue yield; and the fierce feuds,
That long have torn their desolated land,
May (even as storms, that agitate the air,
Drive noxious vapours from the blighted earth)
Serve, all tremendous as they are, to fix
The reign of Reason, Liberty, and Peace!

The Female Exile
Written at Brighthelmstone in Nov. 1792.

November's chill blast on the rough beach is howling,
The surge breaks afar, and then foams to the shore,
Dark clouds o'er the sea gather heavy and scowling,
And the white cliffs re-echo the wild wintry roar.
Beneath that chalk rock, a fair stranger reclining,
Has found on damp sea-weed a cold lonely seat;
Her eyes fill'd with tears, and her heart with repining,
She starts at the billows that burst at her feet.
There, day after day, with an anxious heart heaving,
She watches the waves where they mingle with air;
For the sail which, alas! all her fond hopes deceiving,
May bring only tidings to add to her care.

Loose stream to wild winds those fair flowing tresses,
Once woven with garlands of gay summer flowers;
Her dress unregarded, bespeaks her distresses,
And beauty is blighted by grief's heavy hours.
Her innocent children, unconscious of sorrow,
To seek the gloss'd shell, or the crimson weed stray;

Amused with the present, they heed not to-morrow,
Nor think of the storm that is gathering to-day.
The gilt, fairy ship, with its ribbon sail spreading,
They launch on the salt pool the tide left behind;
Ah! Victims for whom their sad mother is dreading
The multiplied miseries that wait on mankind!
To fair fortune born, she beholds them with anguish,
Now wanderers with her on a once hostile soil,
Perhaps doom'd for life in chill penury to languish,
Or abject dependence, or soul-crushing toil.
But the sea-boat, her hopes and her terrors renewing,
O'er the dim grey horizon now faintly appears;
She flies to the quay, dreading tidings of ruin,
All breathless with haste, half expiring with fears.
Poor mourner! I would that my fortune had left me
The means to alleviate the woes I deplore;
But like thine my hard fate has of affluence bereft me,
I can warm the cold heart of the wretched no more!

The First Swallow

The gorse is yellow on the heath,
The banks with speedwell flowers are gay,
The oaks are budding, and, beneath,
The hawthorn soon will bear the wreath,
The silver wreath, of May.

The welcome guest of settled Spring,
The swallow, too, has come at last;
Just at sunset, when thrushes sing,
I saw her dash with rapid wing,
And hailed her as she passed.

Come, summer visitant, attach
To my reed roof your nest of clay,
And let my ear your music catch,
Low twittering underneath the thatch
At the gray dawn of day.

The Forest Boy

The trees have now hid at the edge of the hurst
The spot where the ruins decay
Of the cottage, where Will of the Woodland was nursed,
And lived so beloved, till the moment accursed
When he went from the woodland away.
Among all the lads of the plough or the fold;
Best esteem'd by the sober and good,
Was Will of the Woodlands; and often the old
Would tell of his frolics, for active and bold
Was William the boy of the wood.
Yet gentle was he, as the breath of the May,

And when sick and declining was laid
The woodman his father, young William away
Would go to the forest to labour all day,
And perform his hard task in his stead.
And when his poor father the forester died,
And his mother was sad, and alone,
He toil'd from the dawn, and at evening he hied
In storm or in snow, or whate'er might betide,
To supply all her wants from the town.

One neighbour they had on the heath to the west,
And no other the cottage was near,
But she would send Phoebe, the child she loved best,
To stay with the widow, thus sad and distress'd,
Her hours of dejection to cheer.
As the buds of wild roses, the cheeks of the maid
Were just tinted with youth's lovely hue,
Her form, like the aspen, wild graces display'd,
And the eyes, over which her luxuriant locks stray'd,
As the skies of the summer were blue.
Still labouring to live, yet reflecting the while,
Young William consider'd his lot;
'Twas hard, yet 'twas honest; and one tender smile
From Phoebe at night overpaid ev'ry toil,
And then all his fatigues were forgot.
By the brook where it glides through the copse of Arbeal,
When to eat his cold fare he reclined,
Then soft from her home his sweet Phoebe would steal,
And bring him wood-strawberries to finish his meal,
And would sit by his side while he dined.
And though when employed in the deep forest glade,
His days have seem'd slowly to move,
Yet Phoebe going home, through the wood-walk has stray'd
To bid him good night! and whatever she said
Was more sweet than the voice of the dove.
Fair Hope, that the lover so fondly believes,
Then repeated each soul-soothing speech,
And touch'd with illusion, that often deceives
The future with light; as the sun through the leaves
Illumines the boughs of the beech.
But once more the tempests of chill winter blow,
To depress and disfigure the earth;
And now ere the dawn, the young woodman must go
To his work in the forest, half buried in snow,
And at night bring home wood for the hearth.

The bridge on the heath by the flood was wash'd down,
And fast fell the sleet and the rain,
The stream to a wild rapid river was grown,
And long might the widow sit sighing alone
Ere sweet Phoebe could see her again.
At the town was a market and now for supplies,

Such as needed her humble abode,
Young William went forth; and his mother with sighs
Watch'd long at the window, with tears in her eyes,
Till he turn'd through the fields to the road.
Then darkness came on; and she heard with affright
The wind every moment more high;
She look'd from the door; not a star lent its light,
But the tempest redoubled the gloom of the night,
And the rain pour'd in sheets from the sky.
The clock in her cottage now mournfully told
The hours that went heavily on;
'Twas midnight: her spirits sank hopeless and cold,
And it seem'd as each blast of wind fearfully told
That long, long would her William be gone.
Then heart-sick and cold to her sad bed she crept,
Yet first made up the fire in the room
To guide his dark steps; but she listen'd and wept,
Or if for a moment forgetful she slept,
Soon she started! and thought he was come.
'Twas morn; and the wind with a hoarse sullen moan
Now seem'd dying away in the wood,
When the poor wretched mother still drooping, alone,
Beheld on the threshold a figure unknown,
In gorgeous apparel who stood.
'Your son is a soldier,' abruptly cried he,
'And a place in our corps has obtain'd,
Nay, be not cast down; you perhaps may soon see
Your William a captain, he now sends by me
The purse he already has gain'd.'

So William entrapp'd 'twixt persuasion and force,
Is embark'd for the isles of the West,
But he seem'd to begin with ill omens his course,
And felt recollection, regret, and remorse
Continually weigh on his breast.
With useless repentance he eagerly eyed
The high coast as it faded from view,
And saw the green hills, on whose northernmost side
Was his own silvan home: and he falter'd, and cried,
'Adieu! ah! for ever adieu!
'Who now, my poor mother, thy life shall sustain,
Since thy son has thus left thee forlorn?
Ah! canst thou forgive me? And not in the pain
Of this cruel desertion, of William complain,
And lament that he ever was born?
'Sweet Phoebe! if ever thy lover was dear,
Now forsake not the cottage of woe,
But comfort my mother; and quiet her fear,
And help her to dry up the vain fruitless tear,
That too long for my absence will flow.
'Yet what if my Phoebe another should wed,
And lament her lost William no more?'

The thought was too cruel; and anguish now sped
The dart of disease. With the brave numerous dead
He has fall'n on the plague-tainted shore.
In the lone village church-yard, the chancel-wall near,
High grass now waves over the spot,
Where the mother of William, unable to bear
His loss, who to her widow'd heart was so dear,
Has both him and her sorrows forgot.
By the brook where it winds through the wood of Arbeal,
Or amid the deep forest, to moan,
The poor wandering Phoebe will silently steal;
The pain of her bosom no reason can heal,
And she loves to indulge it alone.

Her senses are injured; her eyes dim with tears;
She sits by the river and weaves
Reed garlands, against her dear William appears,
Then breathlessly listens, and fancies she hears
His step in the half wither'd leaves.
Ah! such are the miseries to which ye give birth,
Ye statesmen! ne'er dreading a scar;
Who from pictured saloon, or the bright sculptured hearth
Disperse desolation and death through the earth,
When ye let loose the demons of war.

The Horologe Of The Fields

Addressed to a Young Lady, on seeing at the House of an
Acquaintance a magnificent French Timepiece.

For her who owns this splendid toy,
Where use with elegance unites,
Still may its index point to joy,
And moments wing'd with new delights.
Sweet may resound each silver bell,
And never quick returning chime,
Seem in reproving notes to tell,
Of hours mispent, and murder'd time.

Tho' Fortune, Emily, deny
To us these splendid works of art,
The woods, the lawns, the heaths supply
Lessons from Nature to the heart.
In every copse, and shelter'd dell,
Unveil'd to the observant eye,
Are faithful monitors, who tell
How pass the hours and seasons by.
The green robed children of the Spring
Will mark the periods as they pass,
Mingle with leaves Time's feather'd wing,
And bind with flowers his silent glass.

Mark where transparent waters glide,
Soft flowing o'er their tranquil bed;
There, cradled on the dimpling tide,
Nymphæa rests her lovely head.
But conscious of the earliest beam,
She rises from her humid rest,
And sees reflected in the stream
The virgin whiteness of her breast.
Till the bright daystar to the west
Declines, in Ocean's surge to lave,
Then folded in her modest vest,
She slumbers on the rocking wave.

See Hieracium's various tribe,
Of plumy seed and radiate flowers,
The course of Time their blooms describe
And wake or sleep appointed hours.
Broad o'er its imbricated cup
The Goatsbeard spreads its golden rays,
But shuts its cautious petals up,
Retreating from the noon-tide blaze:
Pale as a pensive cloister'd nun
The Bethlem-star, her face unveils,
When o'er the mountain peers the Sun,
But shades it from the vesper gales.

Among the loose and arid sands
The humble Arenaria creeps;
Slowly the purple star expands,
But soon within its calyx sleeps.
And those small bells so lightly ray'd
With young Aurora's rosy hue,
Are to the noon-tide Sun display'd,
But shut their plaits against the dew.
On upland slopes the shepherds mark
The hour, when as the dial true,
Cichorium to the towering Lark,
Lifts her soft eyes, serenely blue.

And thou 'Wee crimson tipped flower,'
Gatherest thy fringed mantle round
Thy bosom, at the closing hour,
When night drops bathe the turfy ground.
Unlike Silene, who declines
The garish noontide's blazing light;
But when the evening crescent shines
Gives all her sweetness to the night.
Thus in each flower and simple bell,
That in our path untrodden lie,
Are sweet remembrancers who tell
How fast the winged moments fly.

Time will steal on with ceaseless pace,
Yet lose we not the fleeting hours,
Who still their fairy footsteps trace,
As light they dance among the flowers.

The Lark's Nest
'Trust only to thyself;' the maxim's sound;
For, tho' life's choicest blessing be a friend,
Friends do not very much abound;
Or, where they happen to be found,
And greatly thou on friendship shouldst depend,
Thou'lt find it will not bear
Much wear and tear;
Nay ! that even kindred, cousin, uncle, brother,
Has each perhaps to mind his own affair;
Attend to thine then; lean not on another.

Esop assures us that the maxim's wise;
And by a tale illustrates his advice:
When April's bright and fickle beams
Saw every feather'd pair
In the green woodlands, or by willowy streams,
Busied in matrimonial schemes;
A Lark, amid the dewy air,
Woo'd, and soon won a favourite fair;
And, in a spot by springing rye protected,
Her labour sometimes shared;
While she, with bents, and wither'd grass collected,
Their humble domicile prepared;
Then, by her duty fix'd, the tender mate
Unwearied prest

Their future progeny beneath her breast;
And little slept, and little ate,
While her gay lover, with a careless heart,
As is the custom of his sex,
Full little recks
The coming family; but like a dart,
From his low homested, with the morning springs;
And far above the floating vapour, sings
At such an height,
That even the shepherd-lad upon the hill,
Hearing his matin note so shrill,
With shaded eyes against the lustre bright,
Scarce sees him twinkling in a flood of light.
But hunger, spite of all her perseverance,
Was one day urgent on his patient bride;
The truant made not his appearance,

That her fond care might be a while supplied,
So, because hunger will not be denied,

She leaves her nest reluctant; and in haste
But just allows herself to taste,
A dew drop, and a few small seeds
Ah ! how her fluttering bosom bleeds,
When the dear cradle she had fondly rear'd
All desolate appear'd !
And ranging wide about the field she saw
A setter huge, whose unrelenting jaw
Had crush'd her half-existing young;
Long o'er her ruin'd hopes the mother hung,
And vainly mourn'd,
Ere from the clouds her wanderer return'd:
Tears justly shed by beauty, who can stand them ?
He heard her plaintive tale with unfeign'd sorrow,

But, as his motto was, 'Nil desperandum,'
Bade her hope better fortune for to-morrow;
Then from the fatal spot afar, they sought
A safer shelter, having bought
Experience, which is always rather dear;
And very near
A grassy headland, in a field of wheat,
They fix'd, with cautious care, their second seat
But this took time; May was already past,
The white thorn had her silver blossoms cast,
And there the Nightingale, to lovely June,
Her last farewell had sung;
No longer reign'd July's intemperate noon,
And high in heaven the reaper's moon,
A little crescent hung,
Ere from their shells appear'd the plumeless young.

Oh ! then with how much tender care,
The busy pair,
Watch'd and provided for the panting brood !
For then, the vagrant of the air,
Soar'd not to meet the morning star,
But, never from the nestlings far,
Explor'd each furrow, every sod for food;
While his more anxious partner tried
From hostile eyes, the helpless group to hide;
Attempting now, with labouring bill, to guide
The enwreathing bindweed round the nest;
Now joy'd to see the cornflower's azure crest
Above it waving, and the cockle grow,
Or poppies throw
Their scarlet curtains round;
While the more humble children of the ground,

Freak'd pansies, fumitory, pimpernel,
Circled with arras light, the secret cell:
But who against all evils can provide ?

Hid, and overshadow'd thus, and fortified,
By teasel, and the scabious' thready disk,
Corn-marygold, and thistles; too much risk
The little household still were doom'd to run,
For the same ardent sun,
Whose beams had drawn up many an idle flower,
To fence the lonely bower,
Had by his powerful heat,
Matured the wheat;
And chang'd of hue, it hung its heavy head,
While every rustling gale that blew along
From neighbouring uplands, brought the rustic song
Of harvest merriment: then full of dread,

Lest, not yet fully fledg'd, her race
The reaper's foot might crush, or reaper's dog might trace,
Or village child, too young to reap or bind,
Loitering around, her hidden treasure find;
The mother bird was bent
To move them, e'er the sickle came more near;
And therefore, when for food abroad she went,
(For now her mate again was on the ramble)
She bade her young report what they should hear:
So the next hour they cried, 'They'll all assemble,
'The farmer's neighbours, with the dawn of light,
'Therefore, dear mother, let us move to night.'
'Fear not, my loves,' said she, 'you need not tremble;
'Trust me, if only neighbours are in question,
'Eat what I bring, and spoil not your digestion
'Or sleep, for this.' Next day away she flew,

And that no neighbour came was very true;
But her returning wings the Larklings knew,
And quivering round her, told, their landlord said,
'Why, John ! the reaping must not be delay'd,
'By peep of day to-morrow we'll begin,
'Since now so many of our kin
'Have promis'd us their help to set about it.'
'Still,' quoth the bird, 'I doubt it;
'The corn will stand to-morrow.' So it prov'd;
The morning's dawn arriv'dbut never saw
Or uncle, cousin, brother, or brother-in-law;
And not a reap-hook mov'd !
Then to his son the angry farmer cried,
'Some folks are little known 'till they are tried;
'Who would have thought we had so few well-wishers !
'What ! neither neighbour Dawes, nor cousin Fishers,

'Nor uncle Betts, nor even my brother Delves,
'Will lend an hand, to help us get the corn in ?
'Well then, let you and me, to-morrow morning,
'E'en try what we can do with it ourselves.'

'Nay,' quoth the Lark, ''tis time then to be gone:
'What a man undertakes himself is done.'
Certes, she was a bird of observation;
For very true it is, that none,
Whatever be his station,
Lord of a province, tenant of a mead,
Whether he fill a cottage, or a throne,
Or guard a flock, or guide a nation,
Is very likely to succeed,
Who manages affairs by deputation.

The Moon

Queen of the silver bow, by thy pale beam
Alone and pensive I delight to stray,
And watch thy shadow trembling in the stream,
Or mark the floating clouds that cross thy way.
And while I gaze, thy mild and placid light
Sheds a soft calm upon my troubled breast;
And oft I think, fair planet of the night,
That in thy orb the wretched may have rest;
The sufferers of the earth perhaps may go,
Released by death, to thy benignant sphere;
And the sad children of despair and woe,
Forget in thee, their cup of sorrow here.
Oh, that I soon may reach thy world serene,
Poor wearied pilgrim in this toiling scene.

The Origin Of Flattery

When Jove, in anger to the sons of the earth,
Bid artful Vulcan give Pandora birth,
And sent the fatal gift which spread below
O'er all the wretched race contagious woe,
Unhappy man, by vice and folly tost,
Found in the storms of life his quiet lost,
While Envy, Avarice, and Ambition, hurl'd
Discord and death around the warring world;
Then the blest peasant left his fields and fold,
And barter'd love and peace for power and gold;
Left his calm cottage and his native plain,
In search of wealth to tempt the faithless main;
Or, braving danger, in the battle stood,
And bathed his savage hands in human blood;
No longer then, his woodland walks among,
The shepherd lad his genuine passion sung,
Or sought at early morn his soul's delight,
Or graved her name upon the bark at night;
To deck her flowing hair no more he wove
The simple wreath, or with ambitious love
Bound his own brow with myrtle or with bay,
But broke his pipe, or threw his crook away.

The nymphs forsaken, other pleasures sought;
Then first for gold their venal hearts were bought,
And nature's blush to sickly art gave place,
And affectation seized the seat of grace:
No more simplicity by sense refined,
Or generous sentiment, possess'd the mind:
No more they felt each other's joy and woe,
And Cupid fled, and hid his useless bow.
But with deep grief propitious Venus pined,
To see the ills which threaten'd womankind;
Ills that she knew her empire would disarm,
And rob her subjects of their sweetest charm;
Good humour's potent influence destroy,
And change for lowering frowns the smile of joy,
Then deeply sighing at the mournful view,
She tried at length what heavenly art could do

To bring back Pleasure to her pensive train,
And vindicate the glories of her reign.
A thousand little loves attend the task,
And bear from Mars's head his radiant casque,
The fair enchantress on its silver bound
Weaved with soft spells her magic cestus round,
Then shaking from her hair ambrosial dew,
Infused fair hope, and expectation new,
And stifled wishes, and persuasive sighs,
And fond belief, and 'eloquence of eyes,
And falt'ring accents, which explain so well
What studied speeches vainly try to tell;
And more pathetic silence, which imparts
Infectious tenderness to feeling hearts;
Soft tones of pity; fascinating smiles;
And Maia's son assisted her with wiles,
And brought gay dreams, fantastic visions brought,
And waved his wand o'er the seducing draught.
Then Zephyr came: to him the goddess cried,
'Go fetch from Flora all her flowery pride
To fill my charm, each scented bud that blows,
And bind my myrtles with her thornless rose;
Then speed thy flight to Gallia's smiling plain,
Where rolls the Loire, the Garonne, and the Seine;
Dip in their waters thy celestial wing,
And the soft dew to fill my chalice bring;
But chiefly tell thy Flora, that to me
She send a bouquet of her fleurs de lys;
That poignant spirit will complete my spell.'
'Tis done: the lovely sorceress says 'tis well.
And now Apollo lends a ray of fire,
The caldron bubbles, and the flames aspire;
The watchful Graces round the circle dance,
With arms entwined to mark the work's advance;
And with full quiver sportive Cupid came,

Temp'ring his favourite arrows in the flame.
Then Venus speaks, the wavering flames retire,
And Zephyr's breath extinguishes the fire.
At length the goddess in the helmet's round
A sweet and subtile spirit duly found,
More soft than oil, than ether more refined,
Of power to cure the woes of womankind,
And call'd it Flattery: balm of female life,
It charms alike the widow, maid, and wife;
Clears the sad brow of virgins in despair,
And smooths the cruel traces left by care;

Bids palsied age with youthful spirit glow,
And hangs May's garlands on December's snow.
Delicious essence! howsoe'er applied,
By what rude nature is thy charm denied?
Some form seducing still thy whisper wears,
Stern Wisdom turns to thee her willing ears,
And Prudery listens and forgets her fears.
The rustic nymph whom rigid aunts restrain,
Condemn'd to dress, and practise airs in vain,
At thy first summons finds her bosom swell,
And bids her crabbed gouvernantes farewell;
While, fired by thee with spirit not her own,
She grows a toast, and rises into ton.
The faded beauty who, with secret pain,
Sees younger charms usurp her envied reign,
By thee assisted, can with smiles behold
The record where her conquests are enroll'd;
And dwelling yet on scenes by memory nursed,
When George the Second reign'd, or George the First;
She sees the shades of ancient beaux arise,
Who swear her eyes exceeded modern eyes,
When poets sung for her, and lovers bled,
And giddy fashion follow'd as she led.
Departed modes appear in long array,
The flowers and flounces of her happier day;
Again her locks the decent fillets bind,
The waving lappet flutters in the wind.
And then comparing with a proud disdain
The more fantastic tastes that now obtain,
She deems ungraceful, trifling and absurd,
The gayer world that moves round George the Third.
Nor thy soft influence will the train refuse,
Who court in distant shades the modest Muse,
Though in a form more pure and more refined,
Thy soothing spirit meets the letter'd mind.
Not death itself thine empire can destroy;
Tow'rds thee, even then, we turn the languid eye;
Still trust in thee to bid our memory bloom,
And scatter roses round the silent tomb.

FROM THE NOVEL OF CELESTINA.

Where cliffs arise by winter crown'd,
And through dark groves of pine around,
Down the deep chasms the snow-fed torrents foam,
Within some hollow, shelter'd from the storms,
The Peasant of the Alps his cottage forms,
And builds his humble, happy home.
Unenvied is the rich domain,
That far beneath him on the plain
Waves its wide harvests and its olive groves;
More dear to him his hut with plantain thatch'd,
Where long his unambitious heart attach'd,
Finds all he wishes, all he loves.
There dwells the mistress of his heart,
And Love , who teaches every art,
Has bid him dress the spot with fondest care;
When borrowing from the vale its fertile soil,
He climbs the precipice with patient toil,
To plant her favourite flowerets there.
With native shrubs, a hardy race,
There the green myrtle finds a place,
And roses there the dewy leaves decline;
While from the crags abrupt, and tangled steeps,
With bloom and fruit the Alpine berry peeps,
And, blushing, mingles with the vine.
His garden's simple produce stored,
Prepared for him by hands adored,
Is all the little luxury he knows.
And by the same dear hands are softly spread,
The Chamois' velvet spoil that forms the bed,
Where in her arms he finds repose.

But absent from the calm abode,
Dark thunder gathers round his road,
Wild raves the wind, the arrowy lightnings flash,
Returning quick the murmuring rocks among,
His faint heart trembling as he winds along;
Alarm'd he listens to the crash
Of rifted ice! Oh, man of woe!
O'er his dear cot a mass of snow,
By the storm sever'd from the cliff above,
Has fallen and buried in its marble breast,
All that for him, lost wretch, the world possest,
His home, his happiness, his love!
Aghast the heart-struck mourner stands,
Glazed are his eyes, convulsed his hands,
O'erwhelming anguish checks his labouring breath;
Crush'd by despair's intolerable weight,
Frantic he seeks the mountain's giddiest height,

And headlong seeks relief in death.
A fate too similar is mine,
But I, in lingering pain repine,
And still my lost felicity deplore;
Cold, cold to me is that dear breast become
Where this poor heart had fondly fix'd its home,
And love and happiness are mine no more.

The Swallow

The gorse is yellow on the heath,
The banks with speedwell flowers are gay,
The oaks are budding; and beneath,
The hawthorn soon will bear the wreath,
The silver wreath of May.
The welcome guest of settled Spring,
The Swallow too is come at last;
Just at sun-set, when thrushes sing,
I saw her dash with rapid wing,
And hail'd her as she pass'd.

Come, summer visitant, attach
To my reed roof your nest of clay,
And let my ear your music catch
Low twittering underneath the thatch
At the gray dawn of day.
As fables tell, an Indian Sage,
The Hindostani woods among,
Could in his desert hermitage,
As if 'twere mark'd in written page,
Translate the wild bird's song.
I wish I did his power possess,
That I might learn, fleet bird, from thee,
What our vain systems only guess,
And know from what wide wilderness
You came across the sea.

I would a little while restrain
Your rapid wing, that I might hear
Whether on clouds that bring the rain,
You sail'd above the western main,
The wind your charioteer.
In Afric, does the sultry gale
Thro' spicy bower, and palmy grove,
Bear the repeated Cuckoo's tale?
Dwells there a time, the wandering Rail
Or the itinerant Dove?
Were you in Asia? O relate,
If there your fabled sister's woes
She seem'd in sorrow to narrate;
Or sings she but to celebrate
Her nuptials with the rose?

I would enquire how journeying long,
The vast and pathless ocean o'er,
You ply again those pinions strong,
And come to build anew among
The scenes you left before;
But if, as colder breezes blow,
Prophetic of the waning year,
You hide, tho' none know when or how,
In the cliff's excavated brow,
And linger torpid here;
Thus lost to life, what favouring dream
Bids you to happier hours awake;
And tells, that dancing in the beam,
The light gnat hovers o'er the stream,
The May-fly on the lake?

Or if, by instinct taught to know
Approaching dearth of insect food;
To isles and willowy aits you go,
And crouding on the pliant bough,
Sink in the dimpling flood:
How learn ye, while the cold waves boom
Your deep and ouzy couch above,
The time when flowers of promise bloom,
And call you from your transient tomb,
To light, and life, and love?
Alas ! how little can be known,
Her sacred veil where Nature draws;
Let baffled Science humbly own,
Her mysteries understood alone,
By Him who gives her laws.

The Truant Dove, From Pilpay

A mountain stream, its channel deep
Beneath a rock's rough base had torn;
The cliff, like a vast castle wall, was steep
By fretting rains in many a crevice worn;
But the fern wav'd there, and the mosses crept,
And o'er the summit, where the wind
Peel'd from their stems the silver rind,
Depending birches wept
There, tufts of broom a footing used to find,

And heath and straggling grass to grow,
And half-way down from roots enwreathing, broke
The branches of a scathed oak,
And seem'd to guard the cave below,
Where each revolving year,
Their twins, two faithful doves were wont to rear;
Choice never join'd a fonder pair;

To each their simple home was dear,
No discord ever enter'd there;
But there the soft affections dwell'd,
And three returning springs beheld
Secure within their fortress high
The little happy family.
'Toujours perdrix, messieurs, ne valent rien'
So did a Gallic monarch once harangue,
And evil was the day whereon our bird

This saying heard,
From certain new acquaintance he had found,
Who at their perfect ease,
Amid a field of peas
Boasted to him, that all the country round,
The wheat, and oats, and barley, rye and tares,
Quite to the neighbouring sea, were theirs;
And theirs the oak, and beech-woods, far and near,
For their right noble owner was a peer,
And they themselves, luxuriantly were stored
In a great dove-coteto amuse my lord !
'Toujours perdrix ne valent rien.' That's strange !
When people once are happy, wherefore change ?
So thought our stock-dove, but communication,
With birds in his new friend's exalted station,
Whose means of information,

And knowledge of all sorts, must be so ample;
Who saw great folks, and follow'd their example,
Made on the dweller of the cave, impression;
And soon, whatever was his best possession,
His sanctuary within the rock's deep breast,
His soft-eyed partner, and her nest,
He thought of with indifference, then with loathing;
So much insipid love was good for nothing.
But sometimes tenderness return'd; his dame
So long belov'd, so mild, so free from blame,
How should he tell her, he had learn'd to cavil
At happiness itself, and longed to travel ?
His heart still smote him, so much wrong to do her,
He knew not how to break the matter to her.
But love, tho' blind himself, makes some discerning;
His frequent absence, and his late returning,

With ruffled plumage, and with alter'd eyes,
His careless short replies,
And to their couplets, coldness or neglect
Had made his gentle wife suspect,
All was not right; but she forbore to teaze him,
Which would but give him an excuse to rove:
She therefore tried by every art to please him,
Endur'd his peevish starts with patient love,

And when (like other husbands from a tavern)
Of his new notions full, he sought his cavern
She with dissembled cheerfulness, 'beguiled
'The thing she was,' and gaily coo-ed and smiled.
'Tis not in this most motley sphere uncommon,
For man, (and so of course more feeble woman)
Most strongly to suspect, what they're pursuing
Will lead them to inevitable ruin,

Yet rush with open eyes to their undoing;
Thus felt the dove; but in the cant of fashion
He talk'd of fate, and of predestination,
And in a grave oration,
He to his much affrighted mate related,
How he, yet slumbering in the egg, was fated,
To gather knowledge, to instruct his kind,
By observation elevate his mind,
And give new impulse to Columbian life;
'If it be so,' exclaim'd his hapless wife,
'It is my fate, to pass my days in pain,
'To mourn your love estrang'd, and mourn in vain;
'Here in our once dear hut, to wake and weep,
'When thy unkindness shall have 'murder'd sleep;'
'And never that dear hut shall I prepare,
'And wait with fondness your arrival there,

'While me, and mine forgetting, you will go
'To some new love.' 'Why, no, I tell you no,
'What shall I say such foolish fears to cure ?
'I only mean to make a little tour,
'Justjust to see the world around me; then
'With new delight, I shall come home again;
'Such tours are quite the rageat my return
'I shall have much to tell, and you to learn;
'Of fashionssome becoming, some grotesque
'Of change of empires, and ideas novel;
'Of buildings, Grecian, Gothic, Arabesque,
'And scenery sublime and picturesque;
'And all these things with pleasure we'll discuss'
'Ah, me ! and what are all these things to us ?'
'So then, you'd have a bird of genius grovel,
'And never see beyond a farmer's hovel ?

'Even the sand-martin, that inferior creature,
'Goes once a year abroad.' 'It is his nature,
'But yours how different once !' and then she sigh'd,
'There was a time, Ah ! would that I had died,
'E'er you so chang'd ! when you'd have perish'd rather
'Than this poor breast should heave a single feather
'With grief and care. And all this cant of fashion
'Would but have rais'd your anger, or compassion,
'O my dear love ! You sought not then to range,

'But on my changeful neck as fell the light,
'You sweetly said, you wish'd no other change
'Than that soft neck could shew; to berries bright
'Of mountain ash, you fondly could compare
'My scarlet feet and bill; my shape and air,
'Ah ! faithless flatterer, did you not declare
'The soul of grace and beauty center'd there ?

'My eyes you said, were opals, brightly pink,
'Enchas'd in onyx; and you seem'd to think,
'Each charm might then the coldest heart enthrall:
'Those charms were mine. Alas ! I gave you all
'Your farthest wanderings then were but to fetch
'The pea, the tare, the beechmast, and the vetch,
'For my repast; within my rocky bower,
'With spleenwort shaded, and the blue-bell's flower,
'For prospects then you never wish'd to roam,
'But the best scenery was our happy home;
'And when, beneath my breast, then fair and young,
'Our first dear pair, our earliest nestlings sprung,
'And weakly, indistinctly, tried to coo
'Were not those moments picturesque to you ?'
'Yes, faith, my dear; and all you say is true.'

'Oh ! hear me then; if thus we have been blest,
'If on these wings it was your joy to rest,
'Love must from habit still new strength be gaining'
'From habit ? 'tis of that, child, I'm complaining
'This everlasting fondness will not be
'For birds of flesh and blood. We sha'nt agree,
'So why dispute ? now prithee don't torment me;
'I shall not long be gone; let that content ye:
'Pshaw ! what a fuss ! Come, no more sighs and groans,
'Keep up your spirits; mind your little ones;
'My journey won't be farmy honour's pledged
'I shall be back again before they're fledged;
'Give me a kiss; and now my dear, adieu !'
So light of heart and plumes, away he flew;
And, as above the sheltering rock he springs,
She listen'd to the echo of his wings;

Those well-known sounds, so soothing heretofore,
Which her heart whisper'd she should hear no more.
Then to her cold and widow'd bed she crept,
Clasp'd her half-orphan'd young, and wept !
Her recreant mate, by other views attracted,
A very different part enacted;
He sought the dove-cote, and was greeted there
With all that's tonish, elegant, and rare,
Among the pigeon tribes; and there the rover
Lived quite in clover !
His jolly comrades now, were blades of spirit;

Their nymphs possess'd most fascinating merit;
Nor fail'd our hero of the rock to prove,
He thought not of inviolable love
To his poor spouse at home. He bow'd and sigh'd,
Now to a fantail's, now a cropper's bride;

Then cow'ring low to a majestic powter,
Declared he should not suffer life without her;
And then with upturn'd eyes, in phrase still humbler,
Implor'd the pity of an almond tumbler;
Next, to a beauteous carrier's feet he'd run,
And lived a week, the captive of a nun:
Thus far in measureless content he revels,
And blest the hour when he began his travels.
Yet some things soon occurr'd not quite so pleasant;
He had observ'd that an unfeeling peasant,
It silence mounting on a ladder high,
Seiz'd certain pigeons just as they could fly,
Who never figur'd more, but in a pie;
That was but aukward; then, his lordship's son
Heard from the groom, that 'twould be famous fun
To try on others his unpractis'd gun;

Their fall, the rattling shot, his nerves perplex'd;
He thought perhaps it might be his turn next.
It has been seen ere now, that, much elated,
To be by some great man caress'd and fêted,
A youth of humble birth, and mind industrious,
Foregoes in evil hour his independance;
And, charm'd to wait upon his friend illustrious,
Gives up his time to flattery and attendance.
His patron, smiling at his folly, lets him
Some newer whim succeeds, and he forgets him.
So fared our bird; his new friend's vacant stare,
Told him he scarce remember'd he was there;
And, when he talk'd of living more securely,
This very dear friend, yawning, answered, 'Surely !
'You are quite right to do what's most expedient,
'So, au revoir !Good bye ! Your most obedient.'

Allies in prosperous fortune thus he prov'd,
And left them, unregretting, unbelov'd;
Yet much his self-love suffer'd by the shock,
And now, his quiet cabin in the rock,
The faithful partner of his every care,
And all the blessings he abandon'd there,
Rush'd on his sickening heart; he felt it yearn,
But pride and shame prevented his return;
So wandering fartherat the close of day
To the high woods he pensive wing'd his way;
But new distress at every turn he found
Struck by an hawk, and stunn'd upon the ground,

He once by miracle escaped; then fled
From a wild cat, and hid his trembling head
Beneath a dock; recovering, on the wind
He rose once more, and left his fears behind;

And, as above the clouds he soar'd, the light
Fell on an inland rock; the radiance bright
Shew'd him his long deserted place of rest,
And thitherward he flew; his throbbing breast
Dwelt on his mate, so gentle, and so wrong'd,
And on his memory throng'd
The happiness he once at home had known;
Then to forgive him earnest to engage her,
And for his errors eager to atone,
Onward he went; but ah ! not yet had flown
Fate's sharpest arrow: to decide a wager,
Two sportsmen shot at our deserter; down
The wind swift wheeling, struggling, still he fell,
Close to the margin of the stream that flow'd
Beneath the foot of his regretted cell,
And the fresh grass was spotted with his blood;

To his dear home he turn'd his languid view,
Deplor'd his folly, while he look'd his last,
And sigh'd a long adieu !
Thither to sip the brook, his nestlings, led
By their still pensive mother, came;
He saw; and murmuring forth her dear lov'd name,
Implor'd her pity, and with shortening breath,
Besought her to forgive him ere his death.
And now, how hard in metre to relate
The tears and tender pity of his mate !
Or with what generous zeal, his faithful moitie
Taught her now feather'd young, with duteous piety,
To aid her, on their mutual wings to bear,
With stork-like care,
Their suffering parent to the rock above;
There, by the best physician, Love,

His wounds were heal'd.His wanderings at an end,
And sober'd quite, the husband, and the friend,
In proof of reformation and contrition,
Gave to his race this prudent admonition;
Advice, which this, our fabling muse, presumes
May benefit the biped without plumes:
'If of domestic peace you are possess'd,
'Learn to believe yourself supremely bless'd;
'And gratefully enjoying your condition,
'Frisk not about, on whims and fancies strange,
'For ten to one, you for the worse will change:
'And 'tis most wise, to check all vain ambition

'By such aspiring pride the angels fell;
'So love your wife, and know when you are well.'

Thirty-Eight
In early youth's unclouded scene,
The brilliant morning of eighteen,
With health and sprightly joy elate
We gazed on life's enchanting spring ,
Nor thought how quickly time would bring
The mournful period Thirty-eight.
Then the starch maid, or matron sage,
Already at the sober age,
We view'd with mingled scorn and hate;
In whose sharp words, or sharper face,
With thoughtless mirth we loved to trace
The sad effects of Thirty-eight.
Till saddening, sickening at the view
We learn'd to dread what Time might do;
And then preferr'd a prayer to Fate
To end our days ere that arrived;
When (power and pleasure long survived)
We met neglect and Thirty-eight.
But time, in spite of wishes, flies
And Fate our simple prayer denies,
And bids us death's own hour await:
The auburn locks are mix'd with grey,
The transient roses fade away,
But reason comes at Thirty-eight.

Her voice the anguish contradicts
That dying vanity inflicts;
Her hand new pleasures can create,
For us she opens to the view
Prospects less bright but far more true,
And bids us smile at Thirty-eight.
No more shall scandal's breath destroy
The social converse we enjoy
With bard or critic tete a tete;
O'er youth's bright blooms her blights shall pour,
But spare the improving friendly hour
That science gives to Thirty-eight.
Stripp'd of their gaudy hues by Truth,
We view the glitt'ring toys of youth,
And blush to think how poor the bait
For which to public scenes we ran
And scorn'd of sober sense the plan
Which gives content at Thirty-eight.
Though Time's inexorable sway
Has torn the myrtle bands away,
For other wreaths 'tis not too late,
The amaranth's purple glow survives,

And still Minerva's olive lives
On the calm brow of Thirty-eight.
With eye more steady we engage
To contemplate approaching age,
And life more justly estimate;
With firmer souls, and stronger powers,
With reason, faith, and friendship ours,
We'll not regret the stealing hours
That lead from Thirty even to Forty-eight.

To The Snowdrop

Like pendent flakes of vegetating snow,
The early herald of the infant year,
Ere yet the adventurous crocus dares to blow,
Beneath the orchard boughs thy buds appear.

While still the cold north-east ungenial lours,
And scarce the hazel in the leafless copse,
Or sallows shew their downy powder'd flowers,
The grass is spangled with thy silver drops.

Yet when those pallid blossoms shall give place
To countless tribes, of richer hue and scent,
Summer's gay blooms, and autumn's yellow race,
I shall thy pale inodorous bells lament.

So journeying onward in life's varying track,
Ev'n while warm youth its bright illusion lends,
Fond memory often with regret looks back
To childhood's pleasures, and to infant friends.

www.ingramcontent.com/pod-product-compliance
Lightning Source LLC
Chambersburg PA
CBHW060144050426
42448CB00010B/2287